蕭山古陶瓷

魏奕倫書於湘之

蕭 山 古 陶 瓷

ANCIENT CERAMICS IN XIAOSHAN

蕭山博物館　編　著

施　加　農　主　編

文物出版社

CULTURAL RELICS PRESS

2007年 · 北京

BEIJING · 2007

封面設計　張希廣
責任印製　王少華
責任編輯　周　成

圖書在版編目（CIP）數據

蕭山古陶瓷／蕭山博物館編．—北京：文物出版社，2007.3
ISBN 978-7-5010-2116-1

Ⅰ.蕭…　Ⅱ.蕭…　Ⅲ.古代陶瓷—蕭山市—圖集
Ⅳ.K876.32

中國版本圖書館 CIP 數據核字（2007）第 021305 號

蕭 山 古 陶 瓷

蕭山博物館　編著

*

文 物 出 版 社 出 版 發 行
北京市東直門內北小街 2 號樓
郵 政 編 碼 ： 1 0 0 0 0 7
http：//www.wenwu.com
E-mail：web@wenwu.com
北京燕泰美術製版印刷有限責任公司印製
新 華 書 店 經 銷

889 × 1194　　1/16　　印張：21
2007 年 3 月第 1 版　　2007 年 3 月第 1 次印刷
ISBN 978-7-5010-2116-1　　定價：叁佰捌拾圓

《蕭山古陶瓷》編輯委員會

顧　　問　張浦生
主　　任　任關甫
副 主 任　李淩峰

主　　編　施加農
編　　委　施加農　趙榮偉　毛曉江
　　　　　朱　倩　吳　健　崔太金
　　　　　張學惠　馬翠蘭　樓黎明

圖版説明　王興海　崔太金　張學惠
　　　　　施加農　蔡敏芳
攝　　影　施加農
題　　簽　鮑賢倫
英文翻譯　盛潔樺

目　録

CONTENTS

彩色圖版目錄

陶 器 篇

瓷器篇

CATALOGUE OF COLOURPLATES

序

張　浦　生

　　陶瓷彙集了人類文明，凝聚著人民的智慧。陶瓷雖作爲生活用品存在，但它的作用遠遠超出了日常工藝品的功能。因爲它具有獨特的觀賞價值，人們可以從中品味和得到啓迪，並獲取廣博的知識與高雅的藝術享受。

　　陶器是全人類所共有，瓷器則爲中國所創造。中國陶器出現的時間約有一萬年以上。中國瓷器從商代的原始瓷開始算起，也已有三千多年的歷史。我國古代陶瓷源遠流長，千形百態，無不見證中華民族燦爛的文明史。古陶瓷是我們祖先遺留下來的智慧和財富，古陶瓷是展示一個地方文明程度高低、文化底蘊厚薄的歷史載體。

　　蕭山是我國古陶瓷的發源地之一。根據最新考古資料表明，蕭山燒製陶瓷的歷史十分悠久，可以追溯到距今八千年的跨湖橋文化時期。在新石器時代早期的跨湖橋遺址出土了大量精美的陶器，品種非常豐富。從質地上看，有夾砂陶、夾炭陶、夾蚌陶。其器型有罐、釜、缽、豆、甑、盤與紡輪等日常用具。浙江是中國青瓷的故鄉。越窯是中國陶瓷史上最具影響的一個窯系。蕭山則是早期越窯青瓷的一個重要搖籃。公元 2001 年 10 月，爲配合 03 省道建設，浙江省文物考古研究所會同蕭山博物館對蕭山進化鎮前山窯址進行了搶救性發掘，意外地揭露了一座春秋、戰國時期原始瓷和印紋硬陶合燒的龍窯遺址。這在我國陶瓷考古史上尚屬首次發現，無疑是一個重大的突破。公元 2005 年，浙江省文物考古研究所與蕭山博物館經過三個多月的搶救性考古發掘，又在蕭山進化鎮席家村安山清理出三座距今兩千多年的戰國時期的龍窯遺存，其中原始瓷的燒製水平已不亞於東漢成熟青瓷。這對研究中國陶瓷發展史，特別是有關中國瓷器的起源，有著極其重要的學術意義。

　　遵循"藏品是博物館的物質基礎"這一法則，蕭山文管會、博物館的幾代人經過不懈努力，已搜集到了歷代陶瓷上千件，其中精品亦有數百件。例如，西周的印紋硬陶罍、春秋的原始瓷鑒、戰國的原始瓷瓿、西晉的越窰青瓷硯、西晉的越窰青瓷虎頭罐、西晉的越窰青瓷男女俑、東晉的越窰青瓷蛙形尊、東晉咸和八年的越窰青瓷槨等文物，無論從歷史價值，還是高超的工藝，都夠得上國家一級藏品的標準。

綜上所述，蕭山的陶瓷文化不僅歷史久遠，內涵博大精深，而且已融入當地人的思想意識和生活習俗中。現經過好幾年的辛勞整理與研究，備受矚目的《蕭山古陶瓷》一書即將付印出版。余有幸應邀擔任該書顧問，優先拜讀了書稿，覺得很有收穫，特此慶賀！在此真誠地企盼蕭山博物館的全體同仁還要與時俱進，進一步做好文物保護工作。爲構建和諧蕭山，促進蕭山經濟發展和社會進步，承擔更多的責任，做出更大的貢獻。

丙戌年春書於南京片瓷山房

Preface

Zhang PuSheng

Ceramics, the culmination of human civilization, are crystallization of people's wisdom. Ceramics serve as household articles, whereas the functions far exceed the role that handicraft articles play. In virtue of ceramics' unique value in visual sense, people are not only enlightened and inspired but also have access to extensive knowledge and elegant artistic enjoyment.

Pottery is the common wealth of humans while chinaware was first manufactured in China. Pottery in China boasts a history of over 10000 years. China's porcelain has enjoyed a history of over 3000 years since proto-porcelain was first made in the Shang Dynasty (1600 ~ 1046 BC). Diversified in category and varied in shape, ceramics of ancient China did not fail to witness the splendid civilization of the Chinese nation. Ancient ceramics are the symbol of wisdom and wealth handed down by our forefathers as well as the historical carrier that mirrors the level of civilization and the profoundity of cultural connotations in a region.

Xiaoshan is one of the birthplaces of ancient ceramics in China. Latest archaeological materials show that the time-honoured history of ceramics fired in Xiaoshan can be traced back to 8000 years ago, the period of the Kuahuqiao Culture. Unearthed from the Kuahuqiao Site in the early Neolithic Age were quantities of exquisite pottery objects in diversified categories. The textures of the objects can be divided into sandy pottery, pottery with charcoal, and pottery with smashed and grind clamshells. The objects are household utensils in varied shape such as jar, cauldron, earthen bowl, *Dou* (stemmed bowl), *Zeng* (rice-steaming utensil), plate, and spinning wheel. Zhejiang is regarded as the hometown of celadon products in China, and the Yue Ware as one of the most influential wares in the history of Chinese ceramics. Xiaoshan is the essential birthplace of early celadon products from the Yue Ware. In construction of the No.3 provincial highway in October 2001, the Archaeological Research Institute of Zhejiang Province together with Xiaoshan Museum conducted a rescue excavation of the Qianshan Kiln Site at Jinhua Town in Xiaoshan. Unexpectedly, a dragon kiln site where proto-porcelain and impressed stoneware had been co-fired during the Spring & Autumn and the Warring States Periods (770 ~ 221 BC), was exposed. It is the first significant breakthrough in the history of ceramics archaeology. Moreover, through 3-month rescue archaeological excavations carried out by the above-mentioned two organizations in 2005, remains of three dragon kilns dating back to the Warring States Period (475 ~ 221 BC) over 2000 years ago were discovered at Anshan of Xijia Village in Jinhua Town, Xiaoshan. The workmanship in firing proto-porcelain of that time turned out to be superior to that in producing celadon during the Eastern Han Dynasty (25 ~ 220 AD). The discovery is of great significance in studies on history of Chinese ceramics, particularly on the origin of Chinese porcelain.

Following the principle that "collections are material basis of a museum", several generations of professionals working with the Administrative Committee of Cultural Heritage Conservation in Xiaoshan and Xiaoshan Museum have made unremitting efforts, which has been paid off by a collection of tens of hundreds of ancient ceramics from past dynasties, including several hundreds of art treasures. For instance, cultural relics such as hard pottery *Lei* (wine vessel) with impressed design of the Western Zhou (1046 ~ 771 BC), proto-porcelain *Jian* (vat holding water to provide reflection of one's face) of the Spring and Autumn Period (770 ~ 476 BC), proto-porcelain *Bu* (vase) of the Warring States Period, celadon inkstone of the Western Jin, celadon jar with tiger-head decoration of the Western Jin (265 ~ 316 AD), celadon figurines of man and woman of the Western Jin, celadon *Zun* (wine vessel) with frog decoration of the Eastern Jin (317 ~ 420 AD), and celadon *Ge* marked the 8th year of Xianhe of the Eastern Jin form the Yue Ware, are up to the standard of first-rate national collections in perspectives of historical value and the superior workmanship.

In general, the ceramics culture in Xiaoshan not only enjoys time-honoured history but also boasts profound connotations, which has integrated into the minds and customs of local people. After several years' studies and sort-out work, Ancient Ceramics in Xiaoshan that has attracted worldwide attention will be sent to the press soon. Honoured to be consultant of the book, I have the pleasure of perusing the manuscript, which has been a rewarding experience. On this occasion, I would like to extend my congratulations on the publication of the book. I sincerely hope that all counterparts of Xiaoshan Museum keep apace with the time in conservation of cultural heritage. Besides, you are expected to shoulder more responsibilities and make greater contributions to enhance the economic and social development for the harmony in Xiaoshan.

Nanjing
Spring 2006

概　　論

　　陶器的出現是人類文明起源的重要象徵。它伴隨著人類歷史的脈絡,成爲人類歷史文化發展最具代表意義的物證。我們的祖先在長期的陶器生產中,還燒製出更爲先進的工藝品種——瓷器。這成爲中華民族的一大發明,爲人類文明的進步作出了巨大的貢獻。由於陶瓷器本身所具備的特有的使用價值與觀賞價值,千百年來它一直是人們最主要的日常生活用具和觀賞陳設品。

　　通常人們所說的成熟瓷器是東漢時期的越窯青瓷。在這種成熟的越窯青瓷出現之前的商周時期,地處江南的浙江一帶的窯工們不斷改進窯爐結構,提高了窯溫,於是就生產出高溫燒製的印紋硬陶和早期的瓷器。早期的瓷器由於胎體淘練不精、吸水率較高、施釉不均匀等缺陷的存在,故而被學術界稱爲"原始瓷"或"原始青瓷"。原始瓷是瓷器的鼻祖。它最早出現於商代,經歷了西周、春秋、戰國和秦漢時期,流傳廣泛,是江南地區人們日用器的主流。原始瓷長期的生產實踐,爲成熟瓷器的出現奠定了技術基礎。浙江是中國瓷器的發源地。早在商周時期,原始瓷與印紋硬陶的窯址就比較集中地分布在蕭山、紹興等古代於越之地。正是如此,東漢時期的成熟瓷器纔能最早出現在寧紹平原一帶的上虞、紹興、蕭山等地區。

　　蕭山位於浙江省中北部,北瀕錢塘江,與古都杭州隔江相望,東鄰歷史文化名城紹興,南接諸暨市,西連富陽市。其西南部爲丘陵地帶,東北面是平原灘塗,總面積爲1492平方公里,屬北亞熱帶季風氣候區南緣,四季分明,雨量充沛,土壤肥沃,人民勤奮,經濟富庶,是典型的江南魚米之鄉。在這片富饒的土地上,曾經孕育出距今八千年的新石器時代早期的跨湖橋文化,各類史前遺存遍佈浦陽江與錢塘江流域。西漢元始二年(公元2年)置縣,名餘暨,屬會稽郡。新王莽始建國元年(公元9年)改餘暨爲餘衍。東漢建武年間(公元25～56年)復稱餘暨。三國吳黃武年間(公元222～229年)更名永興。隋開皇九年(公元589年)廢縣,併入會稽縣(即今紹興)。唐天寶元年(公元742年)定名蕭山,屬會稽郡。

其名沿用至今。公元 1988 年撤縣設市。公元 2001 年撤市設區，屬杭州市。

一

　　據考古資料表明，蕭山製陶的歷史可以追溯到距今八千年的跨湖橋文化時期。在跨湖橋遺址內出土了大量精美的陶器，品種非常豐富，有夾砂陶、夾炭陶和夾蚌陶等。其器型主要有釜、罐、缽、豆、圈足盤、盆、甑以及支座、紡輪、裹手等數種陶質文物。釜的造型有十二種，罐有十一種類型，缽有十七種造型。豆的種類較少，祇有七種。其紋飾有繩紋、交疊的方格紋和菱格紋。繩紋又分爲豎繩紋、斜繩紋和交叉繩紋幾類。交疊的方格紋、菱格紋顯然是用陶拍拍印而成，結合泥條盤築法成型。其製作工藝與商周時期的印紋硬陶完全一致。這讓人們瞭解到印紋硬陶製作成型的工藝方法，至少在距今八千年的跨湖橋文化時期已經出現。大部分陶器的表面都有一層陶衣。黑色陶衣的表面打磨光亮，猶如黑漆，極其精美。部分陶器上還有紅色的陶衣，如缽類器是內飾黑陶衣，外飾紅陶衣。這樣既符合衛生要求，又能滿足審美需求，十分科學合理。在跨湖橋發現的彩陶數量較多，是目前江南地區發現彩陶最多的新石器時代的遺址。據粗略統計，彩陶器（片）佔陶器（片）總數的 2%，佔罐、圈足盤、豆三種陶器（片）數量的 5%。彩陶主要有厚彩與薄彩兩種。厚彩的特徵是乳白色，一般施在陶罐的肩部、圈足器的圈足部位。厚彩的化學成分主要是 SiO_2，佔79.86%，Al_2O_3，佔13.13%。薄彩以紅彩爲主，有的紅彩退色後呈淡黃色。紅彩的化學成分主要是 SiO_2，佔68.76%，Al_2O_3，佔21.42%。所繪的紋飾圖案有太陽紋、鋸齒紋、連珠紋、條帶紋、波折紋、波浪紋、環帶紋、垂掛紋、火燄紋、十字或叉形紋和直綫、折綫組成的矩形紋飾及點彩等。有些陶器的口沿非常規整，胎壁很薄且均勻，甚至還有很明顯的弦紋。很顯然，跨湖橋文化的陶器已經採用輪製技術。在遺址的發掘品和採集到的文物中已發現有爲數不少的製作陶器所用的陶質"裹手"（一說"陶拍"或"填拍"）。這是古代製陶工藝中用"泥條盤築法"製作陶器時所必須的工具，同時也爲跨湖橋人曾經製作陶器提供了佐證。

　　跨湖橋的陶器不僅向世人展示了獨特的文化面貌，也展現了強烈的個性特徵：

　　1、跨湖橋的陶器製作以泥條盤築爲主，輔以分段拼接、貼築，出現了慢輪修正技術。這比以往陶瓷考古界認定的輪製技術出現於大汶口文化時期（公元前4040～2240年），提前了近兩千年。陶器的胎質主要分爲夾砂、夾炭、夾蚌三類，但前者祇是適當攪和了一些砂粒、蚌殻，炭、泥仍是胎質的主要成份。均薄、規整是跨湖橋陶器的另一特徵。從大型的釜、罐，到小型的豆、缽，器壁的厚度均保持在0.5厘米内，厚薄均匀。小型器有突出而精緻的器表裝飾，諸如黑光陶衣、紅衣等。大型器則以規整、均薄取勝。一般内壁有外壁拍打加工留下的密麻、重疊的淺窩墊具痕。

2、跨湖橋陶器以釜、罐、缽、盤、豆爲基本器，綫輪、紡輪則別具特色。陶容器以圜底器、圈足器爲主，平底器少見，不見三足器，説明其時代較早。發達的圈足器及其圈足部位的刻畫、鏤空裝飾，是跨湖橋遺址異於地域其他文化傳統的特徵之一。

3、在跨湖橋陶器的裝飾工藝中，彩陶是最重要的特徵。東南沿海地區的新石器時代遺址中，尚無其他遺址出現如此豐富的彩陶，而且在此遺址的早期就已出現。早期彩陶的主要形式爲盤内彩，表現手法已經較爲成熟。晚期薄彩、厚彩並存，紋樣豐富且規範。從年代上來看，跨湖橋遺址是中國最早出現彩陶的遺址之一。跨湖橋彩陶作彩於陶衣上面，因此陶衣成爲跨湖橋彩陶文化的構成元素。比較特殊的是，陶罐往往在折肩以上施衣作彩，淺盤器則内壁作彩，施彩區的邊緣均以帶彩分隔。這種在渾圓之中進行彩紋佈局的特色體現了跨湖橋彩陶對視覺效果與審美的特殊追求。

跨湖橋遺址出土陶器所體現的許多先進的工藝水平，表明了當地先民對我國古代製陶工藝的發展作出了特殊的貢獻，譜寫了蕭山悠久而燦爛的文化篇章。

二

在《中國陶瓷史》一書中有"蕭山窰"的記載。其名主要來源於蕭山進化地區的茅灣里春秋、戰國時期印紋硬陶和原始瓷窰址。茅灣里窰址位於進化鎮大湯塢村，發現於公元20世紀50年代。它是迄今爲止蕭山境内發現的春秋、戰國時期燒製原始瓷與印紋硬陶窰址的代表。窰址的廢品堆積長達200多米，厚度在1～2米。有部分窰牀暴露，並發現有窰渣、窰具。原始瓷產品以碗、盤、缽、盅等日用餐具爲主，胎質堅密，色灰白，通體施青黃色薄釉，碗、盤、缽的內底多有螺旋紋，也有飾水波紋。印紋硬陶燒結堅硬，胎色多樣，以紫褐或灰色爲多。拍印紋主要有雲雷紋、網格紋、方格紋、回紋和米字紋等。器型多爲罐、罍等。從窯址採集到的春秋、戰國原始瓷標本來分析，它的主要成份爲SiO_2，高達70%～80%左右，Al_2O_3的含量爲13%～30%，Fe_2O_3的含量爲1.3%～3.9%，還有少量的TiO_2、CaO、MgO、K_2O、Na_2O、MnO、P_2O_5等。它的燒成溫度在1200度左右。其表面都帶有一層含量較高的CaO和一定含量的Fe_2O_3青黃色釉。經測試，戰國原始瓷的吸水率普遍較低，最低的達0.16%。這個資料已經超過東漢時期成熟青瓷吸水率的標準，可見其工藝水平已接近成熟瓷器。若不是秦漢戰亂等因素，也許我國成熟瓷器的出現還得提前幾百年。

經過幾十年來的考古調查，文物考古工作者已在蕭山境內發現與茅灣里同時期、同性質的窯址在蕭山進化、所前、浦陽等地區共有數十處。這些窯址幾乎遍佈了當地的山丘，印證了當地至今仍流傳的"周朝天子八百年，個個山頭有窯煙"的民謠。這是目前國內所發現的春秋、戰國時期印紋硬陶與原始瓷窯數量最多的地區。由此而論，我們認爲蕭山的進化、所前等地區很有可能曾經是春秋、戰國時期越國重要的製陶基地之一。首先是政治因素。春秋中晚期，吳越兩國不斷交戰。公元前494年，越國戰敗。三年後，即越王句踐從吳國回越，臥薪嘗膽，通過"十年生聚，十年教訓"的經營努力，終於達到了生產發展、人口增加、庶民殷實、國力強盛的局面，並且訓練了一支"習流二千人，俊士四萬，君子六千，諸禦千人"的精銳部隊，打敗了強大的吳國。公元20世紀80年代末，人們在蕭山湘湖城山之巔發現的越王句踐屯兵抗吳城堡，即越王城遺址，便是那時的遺存。據傳，在蕭山的臨浦通濟還出現了一位爲越王句踐實現"沼吳計劃"的古代傑出美女西施。在當地還存有浣紗溪、貯羅山、西施廟、日思菴(范蠡菴)諸多遺跡。蕭山在春秋、戰國時期曾經處於越國的前哨，是非常重要的戰略要地。據《論衡·書虛篇》記載："餘暨以南屬越，錢塘以北屬吳，錢塘之江兩國之界也。"人們不難想像當年的蕭山大地上曾經金戈鐵馬、浴血奮戰的場面，同時也能借助考古發現，描繪出當年的窯工們忙忙碌碌地生產陶瓷和大量運銷的繁忙景象。其二是地理位置。進化、所前等地與越國都城會稽相距不足20公里。這裏生產的陶瓷能充分滿足都城居民和王室成員的生活使用要求。其三是交通條件。浦陽江、錢塘江横貫境内，水路運輸條件優越。經過錢塘江北上可通吳國，西進直通金(華)、瞿(州)。其四是自然環境。進化、所前地區屬丘陵地帶，有利於龍窯搭建。其間叢林密布，植被茂盛，瓷石、礦藏豐富，有充足的原料和燃料。

建國以來，蕭山本地出土的春秋、戰國墓葬中也是以印紋硬陶和原始瓷器最為多見，是這一時期的代表性器物。

公元 2001 年 10 月，為配合 03 省道的公路建設，浙江省文物考古研究所與蕭山博物館聯合對進化鎮的前山印紋硬陶與原始瓷窯址進行了搶救性考古發掘。前山窯址位於蕭山進化鎮邵家塔村的一座山坡上，發掘面積為 150 平方米，揭露龍窯兩座，獲得了大量原始瓷和印紋硬陶標本。兩座龍窯呈疊壓狀態，是先後修築使用所形成，即後面的龍窯是在前面龍窯廢棄後重新修築而呈疊壓狀。龍窯斜長 13 米，坡度約 15 度。根據龍窯部位及功能的不同，分為火膛和窯室兩部分。火膛的平面呈半圓形，底部由後向前略傾斜。火膛後壁寬 2.3 米，高 0.6 米。後壁距火門 1.5 米。火膛壁以黏土糊面。經過高溫焙燒，火膛內側、後壁和膛底被燒成青灰色的硬面。後壁的燒結程度較高。壁外側呈紅色，紅色土寬 0.11～0.15 米。火膛內填滿了紅燒土及大量灰燼。在火門的外側，即燒火部位，有大量不同大小的圓餅狀泥墊（托珠）。大者直徑 5 厘米，小者直徑僅 1.5 厘米。窯室斜長 11 米，窯底寬 2.3～2.4 米，前後相差不多。窯拱頂已坍塌不存，但窯頂基本平整地倒塌在窯底，燒結的一面朝下覆於窯牀上。窯拱亦以黏土糊成，黏土中摻雜有稻草，頂厚 0.16～0.18 米。窯內頂的燒結面上有枝條綁紮、竹篾編織的痕跡。窯壁以黏土製成。近窯底部因為有護窯土保護，比窯頂略薄，厚 0.12～0.14 米，殘高 0.07～0.2 米。靠窯內一側燒結堅硬呈青黑色且有較厚的窯汗。窯壁自底部逐漸向內弧收，從窯底開始起拱頂，窯壁與窯頂連為一體。窯底輔有沙層，若干部位已燒結成塊，厚 0.08～0.1 米。沙層上不見任何支墊窯具，可能坯件是直接置於窯底燒造的。在揭去窯頂塌塊後，窯底有少量原始瓷殘片與印紋硬陶殘片共存。這表明兩類產品是同窯合燒的。在距火膛後壁約 6.9 米處發現一生燒的原始瓷碗。其後至窯尾部位發現印紋硬陶殘片，未見原始瓷，而其前部多為原始瓷殘片。據此跡象分析，龍窯在同窯燒造這兩類產品時，窯室前段可能主要燒造原始瓷，而窯室後段可能主要用於燒造印紋硬陶。這一發現平息了學術界對原始瓷與印紋硬陶是否合窯同燒的爭論，具有重要的學術意義。前山窯址的印紋硬陶器型比較簡單，祇有罐和罎兩種。其紋飾爲斜方格紋、米篩紋、方格塡綫紋、斜方格紋和菱形塡綫紋等數種，有些是方格紋與米篩紋和斜方格紋與菱形紋組合。原始瓷是前山窰址的另一主要產品，器型有碗、盅、碟、盤和器蓋等，均爲輪製。大部分器物內底有螺旋紋，少量的是水波紋。胎色有灰或灰中偏黃兩種。施青黃色釉，釉層較薄。有些通體施釉，部分施釉不及底。裝燒的方法爲疊壓式，即最底部爲大件器，向上逐漸趨小，兩器之間塡有泥墊（托珠）。據考古發掘的證據來分析，前山窰址可分爲兩期，其年代在春秋中期至戰國初期。前山窰址的發掘是陶瓷窰址考古領域的重大突破。尤其是完整揭露的春秋時代原始瓷和印紋硬陶合燒的龍窰遺跡，在我國陶瓷窰址考古史上尚屬首次發現。這對於春秋、戰國時期窰業生產工藝和龍窰技術發展史的研究具有重要的學術價值。

公元2005年10月至12月，浙江省考古所與蕭山博物館對進化鎮安山窰址進行搶救性考古發掘，挖掘面積達400平方米，揭露龍窰遺跡三處以及大量的印紋硬陶與原始瓷碎片。龍窰由火膛、窰身與窰尾三部分組成。窰長在10米左右，寬度在2米之間。從發掘的情況分析，原始瓷與印紋硬陶也爲同窰合燒。原始瓷器胎釉結合良好，釉面光潔均勻，基本達到燒結的程度。器型主要有碗、盤、盅、碟等類的生活用品。印紋硬陶主要有罐、罎等。器表拍印回紋、方格紋和米字紋。這幾處窰址存在的年代應在春秋中期至戰國早期。此次發掘又爲我國古陶瓷研究提供了更加豐富的春秋、戰國時期燒製陶瓷的實物資料。

公元1989年，長河鎮塘子堰村（今屬杭州市濱江區）一村民挖地時發現了西周墓葬，出土了七十件原始瓷器。其器型基本爲盂、碟和豆三種。一部分盂帶有器蓋，以堆貼S紋或錐刺紋作裝飾。胎體較粗，施釉不勻，胎釉結合較差。釉色多呈醬褐色，少量的呈深綠色。這是當時發現的蕭山境內最早的原始瓷器。公元1991年1月，長河塘子堰山林隊發現了一座戰國墓葬，出土了多件原始瓷和印紋硬陶器。雖然墓葬已被破壞，許多文物被損，但文物的基本面貌清晰可辨。印紋硬陶有罎與罐兩種。原始瓷比較豐富，有罐、洗、提梁盂、碗、盅等。其中的原始瓷雙繫帶環罐，器型規整，造型優美，器壁很薄，施釉及底，胎釉結合較好，是戰國時期原始瓷器的代表作品，經國家文物局專家組鑑定爲國家一級文物。此外，在蕭山的戴村、進化、所前等地西周至戰國時期墓葬中都發現過原始瓷和印紋硬陶器。這説明原始瓷與印紋硬陶器已成爲當時主要的生活用品和喪葬用具。公元2000年5月至6月，浙江省考古所與蕭山博物館聯合在長山進行搶救性考古發掘。這是在蕭山境內首次進行的對商周時期墓葬的考古發掘，獲得了豐富的實物資料。其中共挖掘了十五座西周晚期至戰國早期的墓葬，出土了一百九十三件文物。這些文物全是印紋硬陶與原始瓷，且以原始瓷居多。印紋硬陶多爲大件器物，有罐、罎兩種。原始瓷的品種較爲豐富，主要是碗、盤、碟、杯、盅、缽等日用器皿，還有鼎、簋類的仿青銅器造型的彝器。鼎共發現兩件，分別出土於M1和M5墓葬，造型完全一致。M1出土的器型較大，都爲圓形三足，器身的紋飾是挑剔而成的刺紋，製作工藝相當講究。同墓出土的原始瓷罐，釉色深綠，底飾螺旋紋，肩部飾弦紋、條形錐刺紋加上絞形雙繫，顯現了精湛的工藝水平。其年代在西周晚期至春秋早期。從這次發掘的總體情況來看，有彝器隨葬品的墓葬均爲西周晚期或春秋時期，戰國墓中基本都是日用器皿，其規格明顯不如早期墓葬。

上述情況表明，商周時期蕭山境內的陶瓷業無論是生產方面的窯址，還是出土喪葬用品的墓葬，都已經獲得了豐富的實物資料。但是，這裏還有一些問題需要進一步研究和探索：一是這些在蕭山本地考古發現的西周至春秋早期土墩石室墓出土的數量眾多的原始瓷器和印紋硬陶器，目前在蕭山境內或附近外圍地區還沒有發現窯址。這些產品的產地在何處？這些原始瓷器和印紋硬陶器是否也是出產於蕭山本地或附近地區？蕭山境內或臨近地區是否還會有這一時期的窯址存在？二是蕭山境內這麼集中的春秋、戰國時期印紋硬陶與原始瓷窯址爲何能突然大規模地湧現，且產品的技術水平已經比較成熟？其源頭和技術來源又在何處？很顯然，如此發達的製陶業和製陶技術不可能突然形成，肯定有其根源所在。那麼，春秋、戰國時期影響蕭山製陶的源頭究竟在哪裏？在東周之前蕭山地區是否也有製陶業存在，還是受其他地區的製陶工藝的影響和傳播呢？任何一種文化的出現和形成，必然有其來龍去脈。蕭山東周時期發達的製陶業也同樣離不開這個規律。據目前掌握的考古資料，東周以前的窯址目前祇在浙江境內的上虞、湖州黃梅山和德清的火燒山有發現。其時代約在商末至周初。這些商、周早期窯址與蕭山進化、所前等地的東周窯址是否有淵源關係，還有待於進一步研究。或者說蕭山本地或附近地區是否有東周以前的窯址存在，也得從今後的考古調查中去探尋。

原始瓷從創燒到結束,經過了從商代到戰國千餘年的積累。這爲成熟瓷器的出現奠定了厚實的基礎,也是中國陶瓷史上極其重要的篇章。蕭山境內出土的數量衆多的春秋、戰國時期原始瓷和印紋硬陶窰址,證明了蕭山先民對中國陶瓷業的產生與發展作出了重要的貢獻。

三

兩漢六朝時期是我國古代陶瓷業經過從戰國末至西漢前期的戰亂導致的衰落後又逐漸走向成熟並達到第一個高峰的時期,也是蕭山古代陶瓷業的第二個重要階段。

這一階段早期的漢代窰址在進化的鍾家塢、所前的孔湖、白鹿塘等地已發現了三處。在三處窰址的廢品堆積層中都有印紋硬陶與青瓷器遺物發現。陶器以"泥條盤築法"成型,外部多拍印方形豎條的窗櫺紋與方格交叉紋,火候較低,多呈赭紅色。瓷器施青釉,多爲素面,一般祇在罐的雙繫上飾葉脈紋。從這幾處窰址的工藝水平與質量來看,已明顯不如進化地區春秋、戰國時期窰址的產品。一是胎質粗鬆。從斷面中可看到較多的砂粒,説明原料的粉碎、陶洗和坯泥的揉練不及戰國時期精細。二是釉層較戰國時厚。由於釉中的含鐵量較高,釉色比戰國時的要深,呈青綠或黃褐色。從戰國時期的通體施釉變爲口、肩和內底等處的局部上釉。三是器物的成型也徹底改變了戰國時的拉坯成器、綫割器底的方法,而普遍採用底身分製,然後成器。四是許多產品都是在氧化氣氛中燒成,加上瓷胎中氧化鐵的含量較高,因此多數的原始瓷胎色呈赭紅色。例如,出土於蕭山北幹山烈士陵園工地的西漢原始瓷瓿,雖然器型完整,釉層較厚,但因火候偏低,胎釉中的含鐵量較高,所以胎釉結合較差,釉色偏黃,施釉未及底,露胎處氧化呈赭紅色。在蕭山發現的漢墓數量並不少見,但出土的原始瓷器工藝與上面的瓿基本相同。在西山南麓漢代墓葬出土的原始瓷鼎,在造型上有明顯的楚文化特徵,但其製作工藝極爲粗糙,與春秋、戰國時期的原始瓷器相距甚遠。

秦漢時期的陶瓷業之所以會走向衰落,可能是當時經歷了幾次大的社會動蕩而引起的。一是在公元前 473 年覆滅吳國後,句踐又引兵北上,力圖稱霸中原,並於公元前 468 年遷都山東瑯琊,使會稽失去了政治中心的地位,以至於影響了陶瓷業的生產。二是公元前333年越國被楚國所滅，必然也使陶瓷工業受到一定的影響，同時在陶瓷器的造型中又融合了一些楚文化特徵，故而被學術界稱為"後越文化"。三是公元前222年的秦滅楚。由於戰爭不斷，社會動盪，從而嚴重影響了陶瓷業的生存與發展，致使蕭山的陶瓷業在秦漢時期走向低谷。這一時期也正是我國古代陶瓷發展史上的"衰落期"。直到東漢晚期，社會穩定，經濟發展，蕭山的陶瓷業纔逐步走向興盛。

位於蕭山的東漢晚期至兩晉時期的石蓋、上董青瓷窯址，是蕭山古代陶瓷業走向鼎盛的標誌。石蓋青瓷窯址曾於上世紀50年代被發現，後由於各種原因而被人遺忘。公元2001年初，蕭山博物館工作人員在調查時它纔又被發現。已暴露的廢品堆積長近百米，厚度與深度因表土覆蓋未作試掘而無法斷定。其中所採集的標本有東漢時期的青瓷器碎片，飾有典型的東漢時期的方格交叉紋。西晉、東晉時期的遺物數量最多。其器型主要有罐、洗、缽、碗、盞、硯、燈等。西晉青瓷多有帶狀斜網格紋。東晉青瓷基本都是素面的，並有點彩裝飾。石蓋青瓷窯的標本，無論是東漢的還是兩晉的，其胎色、施釉和釉色都相差無幾。尤其東漢產品的工藝水平已明顯比所前、進化的漢代早期窯址要進步得多。這表明成熟青瓷在蕭山已燒造成功。與石蓋窯相鄰的戴村上董窯址，其時代在東晉至南朝之間，窯址長達200米左右。它燒製的產品主要有缽、碗、盤、盞、洗、燈、硯等生活用品。碗有大有小，均為厚胎、淺腹、捲唇。大碗的內底留有泥點墊珠痕，表明大小碗是套裝疊燒的。東晉產品胎色灰青，施釉較厚，釉色青綠。器物中已出現蓮瓣紋和常見的褐斑點彩，有的盤口壺肩部就飾有覆蓮紋。南朝時期則以蓮瓣紋作為主題裝飾，多數在盤的內心或碗的外壁。南朝青瓷的釉層較東晉時偏薄。蕭山石蓋窯址和上董窯址位於蕭山西南部永興河流域的丘陵地帶。永興河與浦陽江貫通，與蕭紹平原的水網地帶及錢塘江流域相連，交通便捷。六朝時期的蕭山稱永興，隸屬於會稽郡（唐時稱越州，即今紹興市）。永興河流域青瓷窯址的工藝特徵與會稽其他窯口的特徵基本一致，應屬於越窯系列，是唐以前早期越窯的重要組成部分。

在蕭山地區已發現的墓葬中，兩漢時期以原始瓷和陶器居多，其中成熟青瓷的產量還很少。西晉墓葬中越窯青瓷器開始大量出現。除了罐、盤、碗、盞、盤口壺、雞首壺等日用器皿，還多見豬圈、狗圈、羊圈、雞籠、堆塑罐和人物俑等明器。這是西晉時期厚葬風盛行的佐證。公元1991年6月，在蕭山城南聯華村出土的西晉越窯青瓷武士俑和仕女俑，體形較大。武士俑高28.9厘米，仕女俑高26.3厘米，是國內罕見的西晉青瓷人物俑，對研究西晉時期的服飾與喪葬習俗均有重要的學術價值。與人物俑一起出土的還有青瓷堆塑罐、水波紋青瓷盤等文物。同年9月，在發現人物俑墓葬的附近，又發現了西晉墓葬，出土了青瓷豬圈、盤口壺、鐎斗連火盆。其中的豬圈最爲精緻。圈高9厘米，口徑13.8厘米，圓筒形。前門開一方形送食窗，右側上端有一長方形清掃缺口。圈外刻畫一週豎條紋表示柵欄。圈內站一豬，面對送食窗口，神形畢肖。公元1991年9月，昭東鄉的長巷村發現了一座東晉磚室墓。墓室雖早年被盜，但仍清理出九件越窯青瓷器。其中有硯、盤口壺各一件，盞、耳杯連托、榻各兩件，滑石豬一件。公元1995年9月，在衙前山南村航塢山南麓坡底清理出東晉磚室墓一座。該墓早年也曾被盜，清理出越窯青瓷器十一件。其中有雞首壺一件，盤、耳杯連托、盞、缽、榻各兩件。兩墓中均有各兩件耳杯連托出土，且規格、造型特徵和釉色完全一致，應是同時期墓葬。盤口壺高35厘米，口徑16厘米，最大腹徑26厘米，底徑13厘米，器型瘦高，釉色青綠，釉層較厚且肥潤。雞首壺高21.6厘米，腹徑20.4厘米，底徑14.4厘米。盤口，直頸，球腹，凹底。肩置對稱橋形繫，流爲引頸高冠的雞首，圓形喙，通腹，弧形鋬。施青綠色釉，釉層較厚，具有玻璃質感。

　　隋唐時期，越窯的生產中心從會稽往明州（今寧波）一帶轉移。蕭山從先秦至六朝時期長達一千三百多年的製陶史也因此基本結束。蕭山古代陶瓷業前後緜緜相聯千餘年，文化特徵一脈相承，是中國古陶瓷早期發展史上的一個縮影和重要的組成部分，也是今日蕭山極爲珍貴的歷史文化遺產和具有吸引力的歷史文化名片。

四

　　建國以後，尤其是改革、開放以來，蕭山的文物考古工作越來越受到社會各界的關心與支持。蕭山文物管理委員會辦公室、蕭山博物館的工作人員經過多年來的辛勤工作，爲蕭山博物館發掘、徵集和收藏了大量的古陶瓷藏品，從而爲蕭山古代千餘年輝煌而燦爛的陶瓷生產提供了豐富的實物依據，也使古陶瓷成爲蕭山博物館最主要的藏品之一。其總數已逾千件。上至距今八千年的新石器時代跨湖橋文化時期，下到明清時期。其中最具代表性的是商、西周、春秋和戰國時期的印紋硬陶和原始瓷器、西漢時期的原始瓷器、東漢至唐宋時期的越窯青瓷，真可謂精品疊出，玲瑯滿目。

在新石器時代早期的跨湖橋文化遺址出土的彩陶器中，有一件寰底大罐。其肩部飾有四個呈圓形的外圍如鋸齒狀的太陽紋樣。這是跨湖橋文化中較多見的彩陶紋樣，很可能是當時人們對太陽崇拜的一種圖騰。跨湖橋文化中的彩陶主要有赭紅和白兩種顏色，採用白地紅彩與紅地白彩兩種裝飾方法，器型主要有罐、豆幾種。其數量較多，紋樣豐富，技術較爲成熟，是江南地區目前發現最早的彩陶。與其他文化遺址的陶器相比較，跨湖橋文化的陶器在造型上有強烈的個性，而且製作工藝也較爲先進。例如，黑陶器的表面非常光亮，陶器的器壁也很薄。此書收錄的一件黑陶弦紋雙耳罐的口沿處有明顯的弦紋，顯然是已經採用了慢輪成型技術。

數百件商、西周、春秋和戰國時期的印紋硬陶與原始瓷器是蕭山博物館古陶瓷藏品中最具代表性的器物。此書精選了一百三十餘件印紋硬陶與原始瓷器。其中商代的印紋硬陶單柄壺和原始瓷雙繫尊、西周時期的印紋硬陶甕和有著明顯仿青銅器雲雷紋的印紋硬陶罐及原始瓷豆、西周晚期至春秋早期的原始瓷鼎和原始瓷雙繫罐、春秋時期的印紋硬陶雙繫罍和原始瓷鑒以及戰國時期的原始瓿、原始瓷鼎、原始瓷雙繫罐、原始瓷盤、原始瓷雙繫大罐、原始瓷龍、原始瓷錞于、印紋硬陶倉、印紋硬陶帶把罐等都是同時期陶瓷文物中的精品力作。春秋時的原始瓷鑒仿青銅器造型，器型清秀而不失剛骨，釉層飽滿，是春秋時期難得一見的原始瓷精品。戰國時的印紋硬陶倉，倉頂爲圓拱形蓋，倉的中部有一方形窗口，窗口的上下連著梯子。這是一件非常少有的器物，爲研究戰國時期穀倉的造型提供了重要依據。戰國時的原始瓷瓿造型獨特，通體飾S紋，非常精美，顯示了高超的工藝水平。原始瓷雙繫大罐器型飽滿，製作規整，是戰國原始瓷器少有的大件器物。書中收錄的戰國時的幾件原始瓷鼎，是蕭山博物館收藏的戰國原始瓷中數量較多的一種。其中有在蕭山長河塘子堰戰國墓出土的原始瓷鼎，也有一些徵集品，不過都基本出土於蕭山外圍地區。這裏的原始瓷束腰鼎的造型與出土的青銅鼎完全一致。既有青銅器之剛勁，又具原始瓷之靈秀，剛柔相濟。春秋、戰國原始瓷尊也是仿青銅器造型的器物，與紹興鑒湖鎮坡塘獅子山306號戰國墓出土的青銅尊相比，除了腹部的紋飾有差異，其餘的基本一致。很顯然，有很多原始瓷由於是明器，所以其製作工藝與青銅器相比就較爲簡化，但同時也形成了自身的風格。

漢晉、南朝是我國以越窰青瓷爲代表的成熟瓷器出現以來的第一個高峰時期。書中收録的八十餘件館藏精品，也頗具代表性。例如，東漢時期的黑釉五管瓶、成套的黑釉酒具，三國時期的越窰青瓷洗、青瓷虎子、青瓷堆塑罐，西晉時期的越窰青瓷俑、青瓷羊、青瓷硯、青瓷豬圈、青瓷洗和酒具，東晉時期的越窰青瓷蛙形尊、青瓷唾壺、青瓷八繫盤口壺和甌窰青瓷雞首壺等都具有很高的藝術價值。尤其是六件西晉越窰青瓷俑，除了上面已經提到的蕭山城南聯華村出土的兩件青瓷武士俑和仕女俑，另外四件是公元 2002 年的徵集品。其時代可能要晚於前兩件本地出土的俑，體積、尺寸也較前者小。這四件俑的臉部刻畫極其生動，都是面帶笑容，形態傳神，極爲罕見，具有很高的藝術價值。三國時期的青瓷堆塑罐與東漢時的黑釉五管瓶雖然外表色澤不同，後者爲含鐵量較高的黑釉，前者是含鐵量相對較低的青釉，前者比後者多了一些堆塑裝飾，但其基本的造型卻是一脈相承。它們都是葫蘆形狀，四小管的痕跡也非常明顯。兩者相比較，則充分説明了三國時期的堆塑罐完全是由東漢時期的五管瓶演變而來。書中收録的三國東吳時期的青瓷虎子，與江蘇南京出土的有三國東吳"赤烏十四年"銘文的虎子基本相同，應是同期遺物。西晉越窰青瓷三足硯的外形雖小，但工藝卻非常講究。硯臺上佈滿了斜方格紋，蓋紐爲動物造型，用三隻熊作硯足，整體小巧而精緻。東晉越窰青瓷八繫盤口壺，肩部刻畫覆蓮紋，釉色凝重，釉層光亮，有玻璃質感，在東晉越窰青瓷器中頗具代表性。公元 2006 年徵集到的東晉紀年款越窰青瓷槅的底部刻有"咸和八年大歲癸巳九月謝夫人虞氏槅"款。這是目前國内外發現的惟一既有紀年又有"槅"字款的越窰青瓷槅。其意義非同凡響。

隨著越窰中心的東移，南朝以後蕭山的陶瓷業生產也隨之消失。因此，蕭山博物館收藏的唐宋時期的陶瓷器除了部分爲本地出土或傳世品，大多數爲徵集品以及由公安局查没後移交入藏。由於蕭山在隋代一度衰退，人口稀少，隋開皇九年（公元 589 年）廢縣後併入會稽縣（即今紹興），因此在本地發現的隋唐墓非常少。僅在公元 2001 年時在蕭山所前金山上發掘出一座唐墓，出土的文物中有一件越窰青瓷雙繫壺。另外，還有一些本地出土的採集品。五代至北宋時期的越窰青瓷器也有出土，但少有精品。書中收録的這一時期文物多爲徵集品或蕭山公安局查没品。其中唐代的越窰青瓷墓誌罐與青瓷錢氏墓地界碑都是上林湖窰的産品。它們不僅反映了唐代越窰的工藝特徵，還具有一定的史料價值與書法藝術的價值。唐"天佑三年七月八"日紀年款的越窰青瓷盤龍罌是極爲少見的珍品。唐越窰青瓷盤龍罌與上虞市豐惠鎮廟山紀年墓出土的基本相同，也比較珍貴。

古陶瓷文化是蕭山極爲珍貴的歷史文化遺產之一。蕭山古代陶瓷業千餘年的發展史，不僅是中國古代陶瓷史的有機組成部分，也是蕭山古代社會政治、經濟、文化發展的一個縮影。作爲中國古代瓷器發源地之一的蕭山，編寫出版《蕭山古陶瓷》一書，具有非常重要的歷史與現實意義。我們還將在蕭山博物館設立以古代瓷器的出現與發展成熟爲主題的陳列，借助蕭山博物館豐富的古陶瓷藏品，充分展示蕭山悠久而燦爛的古代陶瓷文化史，向世人展現蕭山輝煌的文明歷程。

Overview

Shi JiaNong

Pottery, a significant symbol that marks the origin of human civilization, has become the most typical material evidence with the development of human history . In pottery making activities over a long period of time, our ancestors also created a comparatively superior handicraft work−chinaware, which is one of the greatest inventions of China and has made a great contribution to advancement of human civilization. Owing to the characteristic use value and ornamental value well received among people, ceramics have long been the most important household utensils and display ornaments for thousands of years.

The Yue Ware celadon during the Eastern Han (25 ~ 220 AD) is generally referred to as mature porcelain. During the Shang (1600 ~ 1046 BC) and the Zhou (1046 ~ 256 BC) Dynasties when the mature Yue Ware celadon had not been produced, kilnmen in the neighbourhood of Zhejiang in Southeast China continually improved the structure of kiln furnace so that impressed stoneware and early porcelain were manufactured at high firing temperatures. Due to such defects as insufficiently refined porcelain clay, high moisture absorbency and unevenly applied glaze, porcelain of early stage was called "proto-porcelain" or "proto-celadon" by the academic circles. As the originator of chinaware, proto-porcelain was first made in the Shang Dynasty and gradually became dominant household utensils in Southeast China in the following ages from the Western Zhou (1046 ~ 771 BC), the Spring & Autumn and the Warring States Periods (770 ~ 221 BC), through the Qin (221 ~ 207 BC) and the Han Dynasty (206 BC ~ 220 AD). The development in proto-porcelain manufacturing over a long period of time laid foundations for the appearance of mature porcelain.Zhejiang is the birthplace of porcelain in China. As early as the Shang and Zhou Dynasties, kilns where proto-porcelain and impressed stoneware were manufactured, were mostly distributed at the ancient Yu-Yue such as Xiaoshan and Shaoxing. Hence, mature porcelain in the Eastern Han Dynasty appeared the earliest in Shangyu, Shaoxing, and Xiaoshan within the area of Ningbo-Shaoxing Plain.

Located in the mid-north of Zhejiang Province, Xiaoshan faces the ancient capital city of Hangzhou over the Qiantang River on the north, with the historic and cultural city of Shaoxing on the east, Zhuji on the south, and Fuyang on the west. With hilly land in the southwest, and plains and tidal land in the northeast, Xiaoshan covers a total area of 1492 km^2. Situated on the southern brink of subtropical region with a monsoon climate in the Northern Hemisphere, Xiaoshan is endowed with four distinct seasons, abundant rainfall, fertile land, industrious people and populous economy. Therefore, it is famous as the Land of Fish and Rice in Southeast China. The fertile land nurtured the Kuahuqiao Culture with a history of 8000 years and prehistoric remains of various types can be found all over the Puyang River and the Qiantang River valleys. The history of Xiaoshan as an administrative division goes back to 2 AD during the Western Han when the place was designated as a county named Yuji, under the jurisdiction of Kuaiji Prefecture. In 9 AD, it was renamed Yuyan. The place was called Yuji again under the reign of Jianwu (25 ~ 56 AD) during the Eastern Han. It was renamed Yongxing under the reign of Huangwu (222 ~ 229 AD) during Wu, the Three Kingdoms (222 ~ 280 AD). In 589 AD of the Sui Dynasty (581 ~ 618 AD) when the county administration of the place was abolished, it became part of the Kuaiji County (present Shaoxing). Since 742 AD in the Tang Dynasty (618 ~ 907 AD) when the place was denominated as Xiaoshan under the jurisdiction of Kuaiji Prefecture, the name has been adopted so far. In 1988, it was designated as a city instead of a county. Since 2001 when the city administration was abolished, Xiaoshan has become a district under the jurisdiction of Hangzhou.

I

Archaeological materials indicate that the history of pottery making in Xiaoshan goes back to the 8000-year Kuahuqiao Culture. Unearthed from the Kuahuqiao Site were quantities of exquisite pottery objects in diversified textures including sandy pottery, pottery with charcoal, and pottery with smashed and grind clamshells. The pottery objects are varied in shape such as cauldron, jar, earthen bowl, *Dou* (stemmed bowl), circular-legged plate, basin, *Zeng* (rice-steaming utensil), pottery support, spinning wheel and tool for inner processing of pottery objects. There are 12 types of cauldron, 11 of jar, 17 of earthen bowl, and 7 of *Dou*. Decorations include cord pattern, trellis pattern, and lozenge pattern. Cord pattern is divided into such types as vertical, oblique, and intersecting cord patterns. It is obvious that intersecting trellis pattern and lozenge pattern were impressed with pottery pat and shaped by handbuilding method. The workmanship is entirely the same as that in making impressed stoneware during the Shang and the Zhou Dynasties, from which we learn that the workmanship in shaping impressed stoneware appeared at least in the period of the Kuahuqiao Culture 8,000 years ago. Most pottery objects were decorated with a pottery coating. Lustrous and glossy like black lacquer, black pottery coating was particularly exquisite after polishing. Some objects were decorated with red pottery coating. For instance, earthen bowls were decorated with black pottery coating interiorly and red pottery coating exteriorly. The practice is quite scientifically reasonable because this not only measures up to sanitary requirements but also meets aesthetic needs. With quantities of painted pottery unearthed, Kuahuqiao has been the site of the Neolithic Age where the largest number of painted pottery was discovered in Southeast China. According to rough statistics, painted pottery (shards) takes up 2 % of total pottery (shards) excavations, and up 5% of jar, circular-legged plate and *Dou* shards. Painted pottery is divided into thick and thin coatings mainly. Thick coating is featured by creamy colour, which is usually coated around the shoulder of a pottery jar and the circular leg of a circular-legged object. Chemical ingredients in thick coating consist of 79.86% SiO_2 and 13.13% Al_2O_3. Thin coating is featured by red painting, some of which appears light yellow when red colour has faded. Chemical ingredients of red painting are composed of 68.76% SiO_2 and 21.42% Al_2O_3. Decorations are varied such as sun disc pattern, saw tooth design, connected beads pattern, line pattern, ripple pattern, wave pattern, descending leaf pattern, flame design, "+ "pattern, "×" pattern, rectangle pattern composed of straight and broken lines, or stippling decoration. Quite regular in the rim and thin-walled of fine texture, some pottery even bears distinct bow-string pattern. It is clear that pottery of the Kuahuqiao Culture had adopted the technology that used potter's wheel to mould. Among the excavations and cultural relics collected, quite a few pottery tools for processing the inner wall of pottery objects (denominated as "pottery pat" or "filling pat") were found, which had been necessary tools in shaping pottery by handbuilding in ancient times. The tools serve as powerful evidence that ancient people in Kuahuqiao once manufactured pottery objects in the area.

The pottery objects from the Kuahuqiao Site not only reveal her exceptional cultural profile but also reflect her specific features.

1. Handbuilding was the major pottery-making technique adopted in the area of Kuahuqiao when techniques such as joining together section by section and applied building were supplemented. The technique that used turntable to trim pottery matrix in the area of Kuahuqiao predated the time defined by the ceramic circles that potter's wheel was adopted in the Dawenkou Culture (4040 ~ 2240 BC), by nearly 2000 years. The body textures of the pottery objects include sandy pottery, pottery with charcoal, and pottery with smashed and grind clamshells. Some sand and clamshells were properly added into the former two while charcoal and clay are still major compositions of the body texture. Standardized, well-distributed and eggshell wall of pottery features

another characteristic of pottery objects from the Kuahuqiao Site. No matter it is a large cauldron or jar, a small *Dou* or earthen bowl, the wall of the object is usually well-distributed within 0.5 cm in thickness. Small objects are featured by exquisite exterior decorations such as lustrous black pottery coating and red coating. Large objects are characterized by standardized, well-distributed and eggshell wall. The interior wall is distributed with thickly dotted dents left by a tool used to prop against the inner wall to facilitate patting and trimming for a more regular and well-proportioned exterior wall.

2. Cauldron, jar, earthen bowl, plate, and *Dou* are basic objects from the Kuahuqiao Site. Thread reel and spinning wheel feature a unique style. Pottery utensils mainly include round-base object and circular-legged object while flat-base object is seldom seen. Tripodal objects were not discovered at the site, showing that the shape had existed in a comparatively earlier age. The well-developed circular-legged objects and incising and openwork decorations around the foot are one of the characteristics that make distinction between the Kuahuqiao Site and other cultural traditions in the area.

3. Painted pottery is the most significant feature in decorative techniques of the Kuahuqiao pottery. Painted pottery in such a variety has not been discovered at other sites of the Neolithic Age in coastal areas of the Southeast China. However, painted pottery appeared in the early stage of the Kuahuqiao Site. A major practice in early painted pottery was to paint the interior of an object, which was a comparatively mature technique. In the late period, thin and thick colour coatings co-existed, and decorations were varied and regular. Chronological data indicate that the Kuahuqiao Site is one of the sites where painted pottery appeared the earliest in China. As painted decorations of Kuahuqiao were applied over pottery coatings, pottery coating is an ingredient that consists of painted pottery culture in Kuahuqiao. In particular, pottery coating and painted decorations were usually done on the part above the angular shoulder of a pottery jar or on the inner wall of a shallow plate. The edges of painted sections were mostly separated by striped paintings. The layout that mixes painted decorations in perfectly round objects features the particular pursuit of visual effect and aestheticism reflected in painted pottery of Kuahuqiao.

The advanced technological level reflected in pottery objects from the Kuahuqiao Site shows the exceptional contributions made by local people to development of pottery making techniques in ancient China, revealing the time-honoured pottery making history and splendid chapter of culture in Xiaoshan.

II

"Xiaoshan Kiln" recorded in the book *History of Chinese Ceramics* got its name in the light of the kiln site located at Maowanli of Jinhua, Xiaoshan where impressed stoneware and proto-porcelain were fired during the Spring & Autumn and the Warring States Periods. The Maowanli Kiln Site, located at Datangwu Village in Jinhua Town, was first discovered in the 1950s. It is a typical example among kiln sites discovered so far in Xiaoshan, where proto-porcelain and impressed stoneware were fired during the Spring & Autumn and the Warring States Periods. The deposit of discarded products at the kiln site measures as long as over 200 metres and 1-2 metres in thickness. Part of the kiln bed was exposed, where kiln dregs and kiln tools were discovered. Proto-porcelain products are mainly domestic tableware including bowl, plate, earthen bowl, and cup applied with thin and greenish yellow glaze entirely. The greyish white body is fine and tight in texture. The interior bottoms of bowl, plate and earthen bowl were mostly decorated with spiral design, and some with ripple pattern. Impress stoneware were sintered and solidified with diversified body colours such as purple brown or grey mainly. Stamped decorations mainly include cloud and thunder pattern, net pattern, trellis pattern, rectangular spiral design, and "米" pattern. The objects are mostly jar and jug in shape. Analysis of the proto-porcelain samplings of the Spring & Autumn and the Warring States Periods from the kiln site indicates that the chemical ingredients consist of 70%-80% SiO_2, 13%-30% Al_2O_3, 1.3%-3.9% Fe_2O_3, and a few TiO_2, CaO, MgO, K_2O, Na_2O, MnO, and P_2O_5. The mature temperature is around 1200°C. The surface of the sampling was applied with a greenish yellow glaze containing a high content of CaO and a certain content of Fe_2O_3. After testing, the moisture absorbency of proto-porcelain in the Warring States Period is generally on the lower side, with 0.16% being the lowest value. As the percentage exceeds the moisture absorbency of mature celadon in the Eastern Han Dynasty, the technological level is close to that of mature porcelain. Had it not been for the turmoil of war during the Qin and Han Dynasties, the appearance of mature porcelain in China might have been predated by several hundred years.

Through several decades of archaeological surveys, archaeological professionals have discovered scores of kiln sites at Jinhua, Suoqian and Puyang in Xiaoshan, which were of the same stage and the same type as the kiln site at Maowanli. The kiln sites are almost located over the local hilly land, which confirms the folk rhyme circulated so far: "Under the 800-year reign of the emperors in the Zhou Dynasty, smoke could be seen curling up from kilns on each hilltop." This is also the area where the largest number of kilns firing impressed stoneware and proto-porcelain during the Spring & Autumn and the Warring States Periods has been found in China up to now. Hence, we hold that the areas of Suoqian and Jinhua in Xiaoshan were most probably one of the important pottery manufacturing bases during the Spring & Autumn and the Warring States Periods. First of all, political reasons played the most important part. During the middle and late stage of the Spring and Autumn Period, the two states Wu and Yue were at prolonged war with each other. The Yue was defeated in 494 BC and the Yue King Gou Jian was taken captive by the Wu. Three years later, Gou Jian was set free and return to the Yue. He exerted himself and went all out to make the country prosperous and strong. Later, agricultural activities developed and population increased. Common people became well-off and the country took on a new look with powerful and prosperous national strength. The well-trained crack troops of the Yue finally conquered the powerful Wu. At the end of the 1980s, we discovered the site of the Yue King's city, a castle at the hilltop of Xianghu in Xiaoshan where the Yue King Gou Jian once stationed troops and fought against the Wu. Legend has it that a distinguished beauty named Xi Shi, who assisted the Yue King Gou Jian to realize his plan to besiege the Wu once lived at Tongji in Linpu, Xiaoshan. Quite a few historical sites related to Xi Shi have been found locally. Xiaoshan, once located at the outpost of the Yue during the Spring & Autumn and the Warring States Periods, was a hotly contested strategic point.

It is recorded in *Lunheng Shuxupian* (Discussive Weighing: Chapter of Shuxu): "The south of Yuji belongs to the Yue and the north of Qiantang to the Wu. The river of Qiantang is the boundary between the two states." Therefore, it is not unimaginable that at that time Xiaoshan was once the bloody battlefield where warriors riding on armoured horses fought at close quarters with spears. According to archaeological discoveries, we can depict the scene that kilnmen were engaged in manufacturing porcelain products, which were transported in large quantities for distribution in other regions. The second reason lies in the advantageous geographical location. Kuaiji, both the capital city and political centre of the Yue, was less than 20 kilometres away from Jinhua or Suoqian. Ceramics manufactured here could adequately meet the needs of the city dwellers and the royal family for their daily use. The third reason depends on the convenience in transportation. As the Puyang River and the Qiantang River flow across the region, transportation by water stood out as a favourable condition. North across the Qiantang River stood the Wu and westward was accessible to Jinhua and Quzhou. Last but not least, the natural environment is also essential. The hilly land where Jinhua and Suoqian are located enjoys favourable terrain for putting up dragon kilns. Dense forest, luxuriant vegetation, abundant porcelain clay and mineral resources provide sufficient raw materials and fuels for firing porcelain products.

Since the founding of the People's Republic of China, a majority of impressed stoneware and proto-porcelain during the Spring & Autumn and Warring States Periods has been unearthed from the graves in Xiaoshan, which are typical examples of the stage.

In the construction of the No.3 provincial highway in October 2001, the Archaeological Research Institute of Zhejiang Province together with Xiaoshan Museum carried out a rescue archaeological excavation of the kiln manufacturing impressed stoneware and proto-porcelain at Qianshan, Jinhua. The Qianshan Kiln Site, with an excavated area of 150 m², is located on a hillside at the Shaojiata Village in Jinhua, Xiaoshan. Quantities of proto-porcelain and impressed stoneware samplings were excavated after two dragon kilns were exposed. The two dragon kilns, one on top of another, were set up and put into use successively. That is, the latter was reconstructed at the location where the former had been abandoned. The dragon kiln, in the shape of a slope at an angle of about 15°, measures 13 metres long. The dragon kiln, by different positions and functions, is divided into two parts: a firing chamber and a kiln chamber. The firing chamber takes the shape of a semicircle in its plane figure and the bottom is slanting from the rear to the front. The back wall of the firing chamber, which is 1.5 metres away from the firing door, measures 2.3 metres wide and 0.6 metre high. The wall of the firing chamber was plastered with clay. The inside, the back wall and the bottom of the firing chamber became greenish-grey after being dead-burned at a high temperature. A comparatively high degree of sintering can be seen on the back wall. The outside of the wall looks red and the red clay measures 0.11-0.15 metre in width. The firing chamber is filled with fired lumps of clay and quantities of charcoal ashes. Quantities of pancake-shaped clay pads (strut balls) in different sizes spread at the outside of the firing door. The larger one measures 5 cm in diametre and the smaller one 1.5 cm. The kiln chamber measures 11 metres in its oblique length. The bottom of the kiln is 2.3-2.4 metres in width. The vault of the kiln had already collapsed with no existence. The fallen vault almost rested entirely at the bottom of the kiln. The sintering side covered the kiln bed. The vault, measuring 0.16-0.18 metre in thickness, was plastered with clay mixed with some straw. Traces of bound branches and woven bamboo can be found on the sintering part inside the vault. The kiln wall was built with clay. The wall of the section close to the bottom of the kiln, measuring 0.12-0.14 metre in thickness with a remaining height of 0.07-0.2 metre, is slightly thinner than the vault. The wall inside the kiln became solidified after sintering. The kiln wall gradually became tightened in an arc from the bottom where the vault began to be set up. Therefore, the kiln wall was integrated with the vault into a whole. The bottom was paved with a layer of sand, part of which had sintered into lumps measuring 0.08-0.1 metre in thickness. As no kiln tools for strutting and padding were seen on the sand, green bodies might have been directly arranged at the bottom of the kiln for firing. The removal of the collapsed vault revealed a few shards of proto-porcelain and impressed stoneware at the kiln bottom, which indicates that both categories had been co-fired in the same kiln. A proto-porcelain bowl undergone fast firing was found 6.9 metres from the back wall of the firing chamber. Impressed stoneware shards were discovered in the section from the back wall to the back-end of the kiln, whereas proto-porcelain shards mostly in the front section of the kiln. Therefore, it can be analyzed that, while two categories were co-fired in the same kiln, the front section might have been used mainly for firing proto-porcelain products and the rear section mainly for firing impressed stoneware. The discovery has calmed down the controversies in the academic circles over the opinion whether proto-porcelain and impressed stoneware had been co-fired in the same kiln, which is of academic significance. Jar and jug, two simple shapes of impressed stoneware, were found at the Qianshan Kiln Site. Decorations include rhombic form, sieve pattern, trellis pattern filled with lines, and rhombic form or lozenge pattern filled with lines. Some are combinations of trellis pattern and sieve pattern, or rhombic form and lozenge pattern. Proto-porcelain is another major product at the Qianshan Kiln Site including bowl, cup, saucer, plate, and vessel cover, which were all moulded by potter's wheel. Most objects bear spiral pattern at the bottom and a few, ripple pattern. Body colours are grey or greyish yellow. The bodies were applied with thin and greenish yellow glaze. Some were glazed on the entire body while others were glazed short at the base. During vertical firing, large objects were arranged at the bottom while smaller ones at the top. They were fired layer by layer. Clay pad (strut ball) was placed between two objects. Archaeological surveys show that the Qianshan Kiln Site can be divided into two stages dating back between the mid Spring and Autumn Period and the beginning of the Warring States Period.The excavation of the Qianshan Kiln Site was a significant breakthrough in the archaeological realm of ceramic kiln site. In particular, the entire exposure of the dragon kiln site where proto-porcelain and impressed stoneware were co-fired during the Spring and Autumn Period is the first discovery in archaeological history of ceramic kiln site in China, and is of academic significance in the studies of the kiln industry in the Spring & Autumn and the Warring States Periods and the technological history of dragon kilns.

From October through December 2005, the Archaeological Research Institute of Zhejiang Province together with Xiaoshan Museum conducted a rescue archaeological excavation of the Anshan Kiln Site in Jinhua. The excavated area takes up 400 m², exposing three dragon kiln sites and quantities of impressed stoneware and proto-porcelain shards. Each dragon kiln is composed of three sections: a firing chamber, the main body and the back-end. Each kiln measures about 10 metres long and 2 metres wide. Analysis of the excavation shows that proto-porcelain and impressed stoneware were also co-fired in the same kiln. The body and the glaze of proto-porcelain are well integrated. The glaze is well distributed with smooth finish. The proto-porcelain objects are mainly household vessels such as bowl, plate, cup, saucer, etc. Impressed stoneware is mainly storage vessels like jar and jug, which were stamped with rectangular spiral design, trellis pattern and "米" pattern. The kilns date back to the stage between the mid Spring and Autumn Period through the beginning of the Warring States Period. The excavation has provided us with far richer material objects on ceramics firing during the Spring & Autumn and the Warring States Periods for studies on ancient ceramics in China.

In 1989 when a villager of the Tangziyan Village in Changhe Town (under the jurisdiction of present Binjiang District in Hangzhou) farmed the land, he discovered graves of the Western Zhou Dynasty, and 70 proto-porcelain objects were unearthed. Three basic shapes include *Yu* (broad-mouthed receptacle), saucer and *Dou*. Some vessels of *Yu* with cover were decorated with embossed S pattern and incised design. The body, with rough texture and wavy finish, is inadequately integrated with glaze. The glaze colours are mostly brown and a few dark green. They were the earliest proto-porcelain objects discovered in Xiaoshan at that time. In January 1991, the forest conservation team of Tangziyan, Changhe discovered a grave of the Warring States Period. Several articles of proto-porcelain and impressed stoneware were unearthed. Although the grave had been destroyed and many cultural relics damaged, the rough appearances of the cultural relics could be made out. Impressed stoneware takes the shape of jug and jar. Proto-porcelain objects are diversified in shape such as jar, washer, *He* (container with three legs) with loop handles, bowl, and cup. A proto-porcelain jar with two loop handles is regular in shape and elegant in style. Thin-walled, the proto-porcelain jar is entirely glazed including the base. The body and the glaze are well integrated. The object, a typical example of proto-porcelain objects during the Warring States Period, is rated as the first-class national cultural relic by the expert panel of the State Administration of Cultural Heritage. Moreover, proto-porcelain and impressed stoneware were also discovered in the graves dating back to the period from the Western Zhou Dynasty to the Warring States Period at Daicun, Jinhua, and Suoqian of Xiaoshan. This indicates that proto-porcelain and impressed stoneware had functioned as major household utensils and funerary objects. Between May and June 2000, the Archaeological Research Institute of Zhejiang Province and Xiaoshan Museum conducted a rescue archaeological excavation in Changshan. That was the first archaeological excavation carried out in Xiaoshan of graves in the Shang and Zhou Dynasties. The excavation turned out to be fruitful. Unearthed from the 15 graves between the late Western Zhou Dynasty and the early Warring States Period were 193 articles of cultural relics. All of them are impressed stoneware and proto-porcelain, with the latter taking up a large quantity. Impressed stoneware is mostly large vessels including jar and jug. Proto-porcelain is diversified in category including household utensils such as bowl, plate, saucer, pitcher, cup, and earthen bowl. In addition, bronze-imitated sacrificial vessels such as *Ding* (tripod) and *Gui* (food container) were also discovered. Two articles of *Ding* were unearthed from the graves respectively numbered M1 and M5, with entirely similar shape. The object from M1 is larger. With three round legs, the vessels were decorated with cut and incised design in exquisite workmanship. The proto-porcelain jar from the same grave is glazed dark green, and decorated with spiral design in the base, bowstring and incised stripe pattern in the shoulder. Mirroring exquisite workmanship, the jar dates back to the stage between the late Western Zhou Dynasty and the early Spring and Autumn Period. In view of the overall excavation, graves with sacrificial vessels and funerary objects all date back to the Western Zhou Dynasty or the Spring and Autumn Period. However, the tombs dating back to the Warring States Period revealed some household utensils, which were less luxurious than the earlier graves.

The above-mentioned information shows that the rich material objects from the kiln sites and the graves where funerary objects were unearthed will enable us to study the ceramic industry during the Shang and Zhou Dynasties in Xiaoshan. However, some issues still remain to be further studied and explored. Firstly, since no kiln sites have been discovered in Xiaoshan and its neighbouring regions so far, where is the place of origin of the numerous proto-porcelain and impressed stoneware from the archaeological excavations of graves dating back to the stage between the Western Zhou and the early Spring and Autumn Period? Could these proto-porcelain and impressed stoneware be manufactured in Xiaoshan locally or the neighbouring regions? Is there any kiln site of the same period in Xiaoshan or in the neighbouring regions? Secondly, why were impressed stoneware and proto-porcelain kiln sites during the Spring & Autumn and the Warring States Periods mushrooming on such a large scale in Xiaoshan? Why had the technological level of the products been comparatively mature? Where and how did the technology originate ? It is obvious that such developed ceramic industry and technology did not take shape in one day. Where was the birthplace that affected the ceramics manufacturing in Xiaoshan in the Spring & Autumn and the Warring States Periods? Did ceramic industry exist in Xiaoshan before the Eastern Zhou Dynasty, or was ceramic industry in Xiaoshan affected by the spread of ceramic technology from other regions? The emergence and formation of any culture are bound to have an entire process. Hence, it is the case with the developed ceramic industry in Xiaoshan during the Eastern Zhou Dynasty. According to archaeological materials available so far, kiln sites before the Eastern Zhou Dynasty have been found only in Shangyu, Huangmeishan of Huzhou, and Huoshaoshan of Deqing, Zhejiang. These kiln sites date back to the period between the end of the Shang Dynasty and the beginning of the Zhou Dynasty. Whether these kiln sites of the early Shang and Zhou Dynasties are related to those during the Eastern Zhou Dynasty in Jinhua and Suoqian, Xiaoshan remains to be further studied. Or, whether there is any kiln site dating back to the stage before the Eastern Zhou Dynasty in Xiaoshan or the neighbouring regions remains to be further explored in archaeological surveys in the future.

The over one-thousand-year development in firing proto-porcelain between the Shang Dynasty and the Warring States Period laid solid foundations for the appearance of mature porcelain, which is a significant stage in the history of Chinese ceramics. The numerous kilns in Xiaoshan where proto-porcelain and impressed stoneware were fired in the Spring & Autumn and the Warring States Periods prove that ancient people in Xiaoshan made great contributions to the origin and development of Chinese ceramic industry.

III

Due to prolonged wars, the pottery making industry was declining from the end of the Warring States Period to the early Western Han Dynasty. During the Han Dynasty (206 BC ~ 220 AD) and the Six Dynasties (220 ~ 589 AD), the pottery making industry gradually became mature and finally reached the first peak, which is the second important stage in pottery making industry in ancient Xiaoshan.

We have discovered three kiln sites of the early Han Dynasty at Zhongjiawu in Jinhua, Konghu and Bailutang in Suoqian. Remains of impressed stoneware and celadon objects were discovered from the deposits of discarded products at the three kiln sites. The pottery objects were moulded by handbuilding and impressed with window lattice design and trellis pattern. Fired at a comparatively lower temperature, the objects mostly appear umber. Glazed celadon, the porcelain objects were mostly plain with no decoration. It was common to decorate the two loop handles of a jar with vein design. It can be seen that the technological level and quality of the products from the kilns are inferior to those from the kilns in Jinhua during the Spring & Autumn and the Warring States Periods. Firstly, the texture of the body is rough and loose, and lots of sand can be seen in the cross section. This indicates that the process in smashing and washing of raw materials as well as refining of green body clay was less meticulously done than in the Warring States Period. Secondly, the glaze was thicker than that of the Warring States Period. However, there was a high content of Fe in the glaze so that the glaze colour, usually green or yellowish brown, was darker than that of the Warring States

Period. The body was glazed in such parts as mouth, shoulder and the interior bottom, whereas it was entirely glazed in the Warring States Period. Thirdly, the technology that moulded the base and the body respectively was generally adopted, which completely replaced the technology that moulded greenware and separated the base from the body with thread in the Warring States Period. Fourthly, since lots of products were fired in oxidation state and a high content of Fe_2O_3 was found in the porcelain body, most proto-porcelain bodies look umber. For instance, a proto-porcelain *Bu* (vase) of the Western Han Dynasty unearthed from the construction site of the revolutionary martyrs' cemetery at Beiganshan, Xiaoshan is intact in shape with thick glaze. However, as it was fired at slightly lower temperature and a high content of Fe was found in the glaze applied over the body, the body and the glazed is inadequately integrated, and the glaze colour is slightly yellow. As the base is glaze short, the exposed part of the body appears umber after oxidation. Numerous graves of the Han Dynasty were discovered in Xiaoshan, whereas the technology adopted in the unearthed proto-porcelain products is basically the same as the *Bu* (vase) mentioned above. For example, a proto-porcelain *Ding* unearthed from the grave of the Han Dynasty located at the southern foot of the West Hill bears distinct features of the Chu Culture, whereas the poor workmanship is far inferior to the proto-porcelain products of the Spring & Autumn and the Warring States Periods.

That the pottery making industry declined during the Qin and the Han Dynasties might have resulted from the social turbulence and intranquility. In 473 BC when the Wu fell, the Yue King Gou Jian led the troops to the north, attempting to dominate the Central Plains. In 468 BC when the capital of the state was moved to Langxie in Shandong, Kuaiji lost the status as the political centre, which affected the development of the ceramic industry. In 333 BC when the Yue was defeated by the Chu, the ceramic industry was bound to have been influenced and some characteristics of the Chu Culture were integrated in the style of ceramics, which was called the "Post-Yue Culture" by the academic circles. Later, the Chu was destroyed by the Qin in 222 BC. The successive battles and social turbulence seriously affected the existence and development of the ceramic industry, which brought the pottery making industry in Xiaoshan into an all-time low during the Qin and Han Dynasties. This period was just the "declining stage" in the history of ancient Chinese ceramics. It was not until the late Eastern Han Dynasty that the porcelain making industry in Xiaoshan gradually recovered and went thriving due to social stability and economic development.

The celadon kiln sites located at Shigai and Shangdong, Xiaoshan during the late Eastern Han and the Jin Dynasty (265 ~ 420 AD) marks the heyday of the pottery making industry in ancient Xiaoshan. Discovered in the 1950s, the Shigai celadon kiln site was investigated and found to be groundless, for a variety of reasons. At the beginning of the year 2001, professionals at Xiaoshan Museum discovered the kiln site again while making surveys. The exposed deposit of discarded products measures nearly a hundred metres. As the deposit was covered by surface soil, it was not possible to conduct a trial excavation to determine the thickness and the depth of it. The samplings include celadon shards of the Eastern Han Dynasty, which were decorated with typical trellis pattern at that time. Remains of the Western Jin (265 ~ 316 AD) and Eastern Jin (317 ~ 420 AD) are superior in numbers. The vessels are mainly in the shape of jar, washer, earthen bowl, bowl, cup, inkstone, and lamp. Celadon of the Western Jin was mostly decorated with rhombic forms, whereas celadon of the Eastern Jin was almost plain with stippling decoration. No matter the samplings from the Shigai Celadon Kiln date back to the Eastern Han or the Western and Eastern Jin Dynasties, they are similar in body colour, glaze application and glazed colour. In particular, the workmanship of the products in the Eastern Han was obviously advanced as compared with the kiln sites at Suoqian and Jinhua in the early Han Dynasty, which indicates the successful firing of mature celadon in Xiaoshan.The Shangdong Kiln Site at Dai Village next to the Shigai Kiln dates back to the period between the Eastern Jin and the Southern Dynasty (420 ~ 589 AD). The scope of the kiln site measures about 200 metres. Products fired at the kiln are mainly household utensils such as earthen bowl, bowl, plate, cup, washer, lamp, and inkstone. Large or small in size, the bowls all have thick-walled matrix, shallow belly and curled lips. The bottom of the large bowl bears burning marks left by strut balls, which shows that the large and small bowls were co-fired layer by layer. Products fired in the Eastern Jin are thick-glazed, grayish green in the matrix and glazed celadon. Lotus petal design and brown stippling decoration were applied. Some dish-mouthed jugs were decorated with lotus design in the shoulder. In the Southern Dynasty, lotus petal design was adopted as theme decoration, mostly in the centre of a plate or on the exterior wall of a bowl. However, the celadon glaze in the Southern Dynasty was slightly thinner than that in the Eastern Jin. Both the Shigai Kiln Site and Shangdong Kiln Site are located at the hilly land in the Yongxing River valley in the southwestern part of Xiaoshan. The Yongxing River, linking up the Puyang River and connected with the network of water system on Xiaoshan-Shaoxing Plain and the Qiantang River valley, enjoys convenient transport. During the Six Dynasties, Xiaoshan was called "Yongxing", under the jurisdiction of Kuaiji Prefecture (called Yuezhou in the Tang Dynasty and present Shaoxing). As the workmanship characteristics of the celadon kiln sites in the Yongxing River valley are almost in line with those of the other wares in Kuaiji, the kilns can be regarded as branches of the Yue Ware and are essential part of the early Yue Ware (before the Tang Dynasty).

From the graves of the Han Dynasty discovered in Xiaoshan, proto-porcelain and pottery objects are superior in numbers, showing that mature celadon products were manufactured on a small scale. From the graves of the Western Jin, celadon objects manufactured at the Yue Ware were discovered in large quantities including household utensils such as jar, plate, bowl, cup, dish-mouthed jug, and ewer with chicken-head spout. Besides, funerary objects such as pigsty, doghouse, sheepfold, chicken coop, jar with embossed decoration, and figurine are particularly common, which serve as powerful evidence that lavish funerals were once rampant in the Western Jin. A celadon warrior figurine and a maid of honour figurine unearthed from the Lianhua Village in the south of Xiaoshan in June 1991 are huge-sized. The warrior figurine is 28.9 cm in height and the maid figurine 26.3 cm, which are rare celadon figurines of the Western Jin in China and are of significant value in studies of the attire and funerary rites in the Western Jin. Cultural relics such as a celadon jar with embossed decoration and a celadon plate with ripple pattern were unearthed together with the figurines. In September, close to the grave where the figurines had been discovered, a grave of the Western Jin was discovered. Celadon pigsty, ewer with dish-shape mouth, and *Jiaodou* (warming vessel) and brazier were unearthed. The pigsty, 9 cm in height and 13.8 cm in bore, is the most exquisite in workmanship. Clindrical in shape, the pigsty was designed with a square window for feeding in the front gate, a rectangular opening in the upper right end for cleaning, and a circle of incised stripes outside the pigsty as fences. A pig is standing inside the coop, facing the feeding window, absolutely lifelike. In September 1991, a brick-built tomb was discovered at the Changxiang Village in Zhaodong Township. The tomb had been robbed in early ages, whereas 9 celadon articles of the Yue Ware were sorted out including one inkstone, one ewer with dish-shaped mouth, two small cups, two handled cups with trays, two *Ge*(food container), and one talcum pig. In September 1995, a brick tomb was sorted out at the bottom of the southern foot of Hangwu Hill, Yaqian. The tomb had also been robbed in early ages. Eleven celadon articles of the Yue Ware were sorted out including one ewer with chicken-head spout, two plates, two handled cups with trays, two small cups, two earthen bowls, and two *Ge*. The two handled cups with trays unearthed from the above-mentioned two tombs respectively are in complete conformity in specifications, moulding features and glazed colours, which indicate that they are of the same stage. The ewer with dish-shaped mouth measures 35 cm in height, 16 cm in bore, 26 cm in maxium belly diametre, and 13 cm in base diametre. The slim object is glazed with thick and lustrous celadon. The ewer with chicken-head spout measures 21.6 cm in height, 20.4 cm in belly diametre, and 14.4 cm in base diametre. With dish-shaped mouth, straight neck, swelling belly, concave base, round spout and arc loop handles in the shoulder, the ewer is glazed with thick celadon like the texture of glass.

During the Sui (581 ~ 618 AD) and the Tang (618 ~ 907 AD) Dynasties, the production centre of the Yue Ware gradually moved to Mingzhou (present Ningbo) from Kuaiji. The pottery making history of over 1300 years between the stage before the Qin Dynasty and the Six Dynasties in ancient Xiaoshan almost came to an end. The over 1000-year pottery making history in ancient Xiaoshan can be traced back to the same origin of cultural features,which is not only an epitome and essential ingredient in the early development of ancient Chinese ceramic hostory but also regarded as valuable historical and cultural heritage and an appealing historical and cultural card of Xiaoshan today.

IV

Since the founding of the People's Repulic of China, particularly the implementation of the reform and open policy, the heritage conservation and archaeological work in Xiaoshan have attracted more and more attention and support from various circles of the society. The professionals working with the Administrative Committee of Cultural Heritage Conservation in Xiaoshan and Xiaoshan Museum have excavated and acquired large quantities of ancient ceramic products through years' hard work for Xiaoshan Museum. Hence, the brilliant pottery making history in Xiaoshan is enriched with important material evidence. Ancient ceramics have become one of the most essential collections in Xiaoshan Museum. The ceramics collection totally amounts to as many as over one thousand articles dating back to the stage between the 8000-year Kuahuqiao Culture in the Neolithic Age and the Ming (1368 ~ 1644 AD) and Qing (1644 ~ 1911 AD) Dynasties. The endless array of the superb collection dazzles people with most typical objects such as impressed stoneware and proto-porcelain of the Shang, the Western Zhou , the Spring & Autumn and Warring States Periods, proto-porcelain of the Western Han, the Yue Ware celadon of the Eastern Han and the Tang and Song (960 ~ 1279 AD) Dynasties.

Of the huge painted pottery articles unearthed from the Kuahuqiao Site, there is a large jar with round base, which is decorated with four sawtooth-rimmed sun discs design in the shoulder. This type of decoration is quite common in painted pottery from the Kuahuqiao Site. The pattern was more likely regarded as a totem by ancient people to show their worship of the sun. Umber and white were two major paints used to decorate the pottery at the Kuahuqiao Site. There were two decorative methods: red paint over white ground, and white paint over red ground. Objects are mainly in the shape of jar and *Dou*. Varied in decoration and mature in workmanship, the numerous painted pottery is the earliest ever discovered in Southeast China. Compared with pottery from other cultural sites, pottery from the Kuahuqiao Site enjoys strong individuality in shape and boasts advanced workmanship. For instance, black pottery is glossy and thin-walled. A black pottery jar with two loop handles illustrated in the book was decorated with marked bow-string pattern in the rim. It is clear that the technique that used turntable to mould was adopted at that time.

Tens of hundreds of impressed stoneware and proto-porcelain of the Shang, the Western Zhou, the Spring & Autumn and Warring States Periods are typical objects collected by Xiaoshan Museum. Over 130 selected articles including impressed stoneware and proto-porcelain have been included in the book. For instance, hard pottery ewer with stamped design and proto-porcelain *Zun* (wine vessel) of the Shang Dynasty; hard pottery *Weng* (urn with a big belly) with stamped design, bronze-imitated hard pottery jar with impressed cloud and thunder pattern and proto-porcelain *Dou* (stemmed bowl) of the Western Zhou; proto-porcelain *Ding* and proto-porcelain jar with two loop handles between the late Western Zhou and the early Spring & Autumn Period; hard pottery *Sheng* (measuring vessel) with two loop handles and proto-porcelain *Jian* (vat) of the Spring & Autumn Period; proto-porcelain *Bu* (vase) , proto-porcelain *Ding* , proto-porcelain jar with two loop handles, proto-porcelain plates, large proto-porcelain jar with two loop handles, proto-porcelain dragon, proto-porcelain Chun Yu(military musical instrument), hard pottery barn with textile impression, and hard pottery ewers with textile impression of the Warring States Period. The proto-porcelain *Jian* of the Spring & Autumn Period, a bronze imitation, is elegant and vigorous in shape with lustrous glaze, which is a rare art treasure of the Spring & Autumn Period. The hard pottery barn with textile impression of the Spring & Autumn Period is facilitated with a vault, a square window in the middle of the vault, and a ladder that links the upper and lower parts of the window. The object has provided us with important evidence for studies on the shape of barn in the Warring States Period. Unique in style, the proto-porcelain *Bu* with cover of the Warring States Period is entirely decorated with exquisite "S" pattern, reflecting superb workmanship. The large proto-porcelain jar with two loop handles is plump in shape and regular in workmanship, which is a large one rarely seen among proto-porcelain objects of the Warring States Period. The proto-porcelain *Dings* of the Warring States Period illustrated in the book are among the numerous proto-porcelain *Dings* of the Warring States Period collected at Xiaoshan Museum. For instance, the proto-porcelain *Ding* unearthed locally from the tomb during the Warring States Period in Tangziyan, Changhe and some were acquisitions. They were mostly unearthed from Xiaoshan or its neighbouring regions. The proto-porcelain *Ding* with tightened belly, entirely in conformity with unearthed bronze *Ding* in shape, is a combination of the vigorous style of bronzeware and elegance of proto-porcelain. The proto-porcelain *Zun* of the Spring & Autumn and Warring States Periods is also a bronze imitation, which is almost in conformity with the bronze *Zun* unearthed from the Warring States Period tomb No. 306 at Lion Hill in Jianhu, Shaoxing except for the different decorations in the bellies. It is clear that when proto-porcelain objects were used as funerary objects, the workmanship became more simplified than that in making bronzeware, forming its own style.

It was during the Han, Jin and Southern Dynasties that mature celadon from the Yue Ware reached the first peak. The over 80 art treasures illustrated in the book are typical examples with high artistic value such as black-glazed vase with five tubular protrusions, set of black-glazed wine vessels of the Eastern Han; celadon tripodal washer, celadon chamber pot and celadon jar with embossed decoration from the Yue Ware of the Three Kingdoms Period; celadon figures, celadon ram, celadon inkstone, celadon pigsty, celadon washers and wine vessels from the Yue Ware of the Western Jin; celadon *Zun* with frog decoration, celadon spittoon, celadon jar with dish mouth and eight loop handles from the Yue Ware, and celadon ewer with chicken-head spout from the Ou Ware of the Eastern Jin. In particular, of the six celadon figures from the Yue Ware of the Western Jin, four articles were acquired in 2002 whereas the other two had been unearthed at the Lianhua Village in the south of Xiaoshan. The age of the four acquisitions is later than the two articles unearthed locally and the measurements of the four are smaller. However, the four figures are vivid and lifelike with smiling facial expression, which are of high artistic value. The glazed colour of the celadon jar with embossed decoration of the Three Kingdoms Period (220 ~ 265 AD) is different from that of the black-glazed vase with five tubular protrusions of the Eastern Han. The latter is glazed black with a high content of Fe, whereas the former glazed celadon with a comparatively lower content of Fe. Although the former is decorated with less embossed design, both objects are gourd-shaped with distinct trace of tubular protrusions. In comparison, there is adequate evidence that the celadon jar with embossed decoration of the Three Kingdoms Period evolved from the vase with five tubular protrusions of the Eastern Han. The celadon chamber pot of the Three Kingdoms Period illustrated in the book, basically the same as the one inscribed "the 14th year of Chiwu" unearthed from Nanjing, Jiangsu, should have been the remains of the Eastern Wu (222 ~ 280 AD). The celadon inkstone with three legs from the Yue Ware of the Western Jin is not large in shape but exquisite in workmanship. The cover is decorated with rhombic form. The cover knob is animal shaped and the three legs are bear shaped. The entire inkstone is delicate and fine. The dish-mouthed celadon jar with eight loop handles is incised with lotus pattern in the shoulder. The object is applied with thick, glossy and lustrous glaze like the texture of glass, which is a typical example among celadon objects from the Yue Ware of the Eastern Jin. Two celadon *Ge* with reign marks from the Yue Ware of the Eastern Jin acquired in 2006, bear the characters "Specially Made Ge for Mrs Xie whose family name is Yu in the 8th year of Xianhe" on the base. They are the only ones from the Yue Ware bearing both reign mark and the character "*Ge*" discovered so far, which is of unusual significance.

When the production centre of the Yue Ware moved eastward, the ceramic industry in Xiaoshan disappeared after the Southern Dynasty. Therefore, the ceramic objects manufactured during the Tang and Song Dynasties collected at Xiaoshan Museum were partly produced locally or handed down from ancient times. However, most were acquisitions or confiscation by public security organs and turned over to the museum. As Xiaoshan once declined and was sparsely populated in the Sui Dynasty, it became part of Kuaiji (present Shaoxing) in 589 AD when the county administration was abolished. Hence, few tombs of the Sui and the Tang Dynasties were discovered locally. It was only in 2001 that a Tang Dynasty tomb was excavated at Jinshan, Suoqian. A celadon jug with two loop handles from the Yue Ware was discovered among the cultural relics unearthed. Besides, there are some samplings unearthed locally. Few art treasures were found among the unearthed celadon objects from the Yue Ware between the Five Dynasties (907 ~ 960 AD) and Northern Song Dynasty (960 ~ 1127 AD). The cultural relics of this stage collected in the book are mostly acquisitions or confiscation by public security organs in Xiaoshan. A celadon jar with epitaph and a celadon boundary tablet of the Qian's tomb from the Yue Ware of the Tang Dynasty were both produced at the kilns in Shanglinhu, which not only mirror the technological features of the Yue Ware in the Tang Dynasty, but also are of historical and calligraphical value. The Tang Dynasty *Ying* (round jar with a small opening) with coiled dragon design and the reign mark "the 8th of July in the 3rd year of Tianyou" is a rare art treasure. The Tang Dynasty celadon *Ying* with coiled dragon design from the Yue Ware is almost the same as the one unearthed from the tomb with reign mark in Miaoshan of Fenghui Town, Shangyu, which is also very precious.

Ancient ceramic culture is one of the most typical historical and cultural heritage in Xiaoshan. The thousand-year development of ancient ceramic industry in Xiaoshan is not only an essential ingredient of Chinese ceramic history, but also an epitome of political, economic and cultural development in ancient Xiaoshan. It is of historical and practical significance to compile and publish *Ancient Ceramics in Xiaoshan* because Xiaoshan is one of the birthplaces of ancient Chinese porcelain products. Meanwhile, we are planning a thematic exhibition at Xiaoshan Museum, focusing on the origin, development and maturity of ancient ceramics. Therefore, the wealth of ancient ceramics collection at the museum will fully showcase the time-honoured and brilliant history of ceramic culture and present before people's eyes the resplendent civilisation in Xiaoshan.

彩 色 圖 版
COLOURPLATES

一　黑陶豆　跨湖橋文化

1. Black Pottery *Dou* (stemmed bowl)　　*Kuahuqiao Culture(6000 ~ 5000 BC)*

二　黑陶豆　跨湖橋文化
2. Black Pottery *Dou* (stemmed bowl)　*Kuahuqiao Culture(6000 ~ 5000 BC)*

三　黑陶弦紋雙耳罐　跨湖橋文化

3. Two-handled Black Pottery Jar with Bow-String Design　*Kuahuqiao Culture(6000 ~ 5000 BC)*

四　紅衣灰陶雙耳折腹罐　跨湖橋文化

4. Two-handled Grey Pottery Jar Painted Red　*Kuahuqiao Culture(6000 ~ 5000 BC)*

五　紅衣黑裏陶缽　跨湖橋文化

5. Black Pottery *Bo* (small basin-shaped container) Painted Red　*Kuahuqiao Culture(6000 ~ 5000 BC)*

六　紅衣灰陶豆　跨湖橋文化
6. Grey Pottery *Dou* (stemmed bowl) Painted Red　*Kuahuqiao Culture(6000 ~ 5000 BC)*

七　黑陶雙耳罐　跨湖橋文化

7. Two-handled Black Pottery Jar　*Kuahuqiao Culture(6000 ~ 5000 BC)*

八　太陽紋彩陶片　跨湖橋文化

8. Painted Pottery Shard with Sun Motif

Kuahuqiao Culture(6000 ~ 5000 BC)

九 灰陶支座 跨湖橋文化

9. Grey Pottery Support   *Kuahuqiao Culture(6000 ~ 5000 BC)*

一〇　灰陶裏手　跨湖橋文化
10. Grey Pottery Tool for Inner Processing　*Kuahuqiao Culture(6000 ~ 5000 BC)*

一一　印紋硬陶提梁盉　商

11. Loop-handled Hard Pottery *He* (tripodal container for holding wine) with Stamped Design

　　Shang (1600 ~ 1046 BC)

一三　印紋硬陶單柄壺　商

13 .Hard Pottery Ewer with a Handle and Stamped Design　*Shang (1600 ~ 1046 BC)*

一四　硬陶雙耳尊　商
14. Two-handled Hard Pottery *Zun* (wine vessel)　　*Shang (1600 ~ 1046 BC)*

一五　印紋硬陶雙耳罐　商

15. Two-handled Hard Pottery Jar with Stamped Design　*Shang (1600 ~ 1046 BC)*

一六　印紋硬陶罐　商晚期至西周早期

16 .Hard Pottery Jar with Stamped Design　*Late Shang ～ EarlyWestern Zhou (1147 ～ 977 BC)*

一七　印紋硬陶尊　西周

17. Hard Pottery *Zun* (wine vessel) with Stamped Design　*Western Zhou (1046 ~ 771 BC)*

一八　印紋硬陶罐　西周

18. Hard Pottery Jar with Stamped Design　*Western Zhou (1046 ~ 771 BC)*

一九　印紋硬陶罐　西周

19.Hard Pottery Jar with Stamped Design　*Western Zhou (1046 ~ 771 BC)*

二〇　印紋硬陶罍　西周
20. Hard Pottery *Lei* (wine vessel) with Stamped Design　*Western Zhou (1046 ~ 771 BC)*

二一　印紋硬陶罍　西周

21. Hard Pottery *Lei* (wine vessel) with Stamped Design　*Western Zhou (1046 ~ 771 BC)*

二二　印紋硬陶罍　西周
22. Hard Pottery *Lei* (wine vessel) with Stamped Design　*Western Zhou (1046 ~ 771 BC)*

二四　印紋硬陶三繫罐　西周

24. Hard Pottery Jar with Stamped Design and Three Loop Handles　*Western Zhou (1046～771 BC)*

二三　印紋硬陶甕　西周

23. Hard Pottery *Weng* (urn with a big belly) with Stamped Design　*Western Zhou (1046～771 BC)*

二五　印紋硬陶罐　西周

25. Hard Pottery Jar with Stamped Design　*Western Zhou (1046 ~ 771 BC)*

二六　印紋硬陶罐　西周
26. Hard Pottery Jar with Stamped Design　*Western Zhou (1046 ~ 771 BC)*

二七　印紋硬陶雙繫罐　西周
27. Hard Pottery Jar with Stamped Design and Two Loop Handles　*Western Zhou (1046 ~ 771 BC)*

二八　印紋硬陶獸耳罐　西周
28. Hard Pottery Jar with Stamped
　　Design and Animal-shaped Handles
　　Western Zhou (1046 ~ 771 BC)

二九　印紋硬陶雙耳罐　西周

29. Two-handled Hard Pottery Jug with Stamped Design　*Western Zhou (1046 ~ 771 BC)*

三〇　印紋硬陶獸耳罍　西周

30. Hard Pottery Jug with Stamped Design and Animal-shaped Handles　*Western Zhou (1046 ~ 771 BC)*

三一　印紋硬陶罐　春秋

31. Hard Pottery Jar with Stamped Design　*Spring & Autumn Period (770 ~ 476 BC)*

三二　印紋硬陶雙耳壺　春秋

32. Two-handled Hard Pottery Ewer with Stamped Design　*Spring & Autumn Period (770 ~ 476 BC)*

73

三三　印紋硬陶雙繫罐　春秋

33.Hard Pottery Jar with Stamped Design and Two Loop Handles　*Spring & Autumn Period (770 ~ 476 BC)*

三四　印紋硬陶雙耳罐　春秋

34. Two-handled Hard Pottery Jar with Stamped Design　*Spring & Autumn Period(770 ~ 476 BC)*

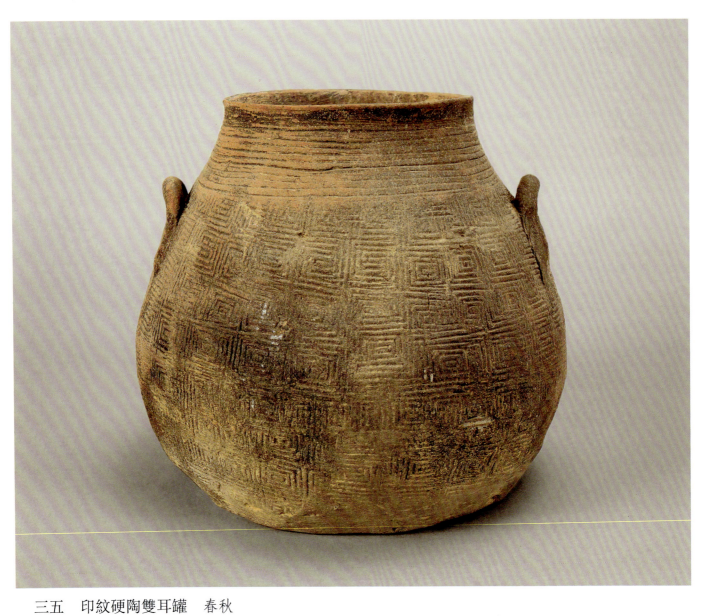

三五　印紋硬陶雙耳罐　春秋

35. Two-handled Hard Pottery Jar with Stamped Design　*Spring & Autumn Period (770 ~ 476 BC)*

三六　印紋硬陶三繫罐　春秋

36. Hard Pottery Jar with Stamped Design and Three Loop Handles　*Spring & Autumn Period (770 ~ 476 BC)*

三七　印紋硬陶罐　春秋
37. Hard Pottery Jar with Stamped Design　*Spring & Autumn Period (770 ~ 476 BC)*

四〇　印紋硬陶雙繫罐　春秋
40. Hard Pottery Jar with Stamped Design and Two Loop Handles　*Spring & Autumn Period (770 ~ 476 BC)*

三九　印紋硬陶罌　春秋
39.Hard Pottery Jug with Stamped Design　*Spring & Autumn Period (770 ~ 476 BC)*

四二　印紋硬陶雙繋壺　春秋
42. Hard Pottery Ewer with Stamped Design and Two Loop Handles　*Spring & Autumn Period (770 ~ 476 BC)*

四一　印紋硬陶人物紋罐　春秋
41. Hard Pottery Jar with Stamped Design and Figures　*Spring & Autumn Period (770 ~ 476 BC)*

四三　印紋硬陶罐　春秋

43. Hard Pottery Jar with Stamped Design　*Spring & Autumn Period (770～476 BC)*

四四　印紋硬陶罐　春秋
44. Hard Pottery Jar with Stamped Design　*Spring & Autumn Period (770 ~ 476 BC)*

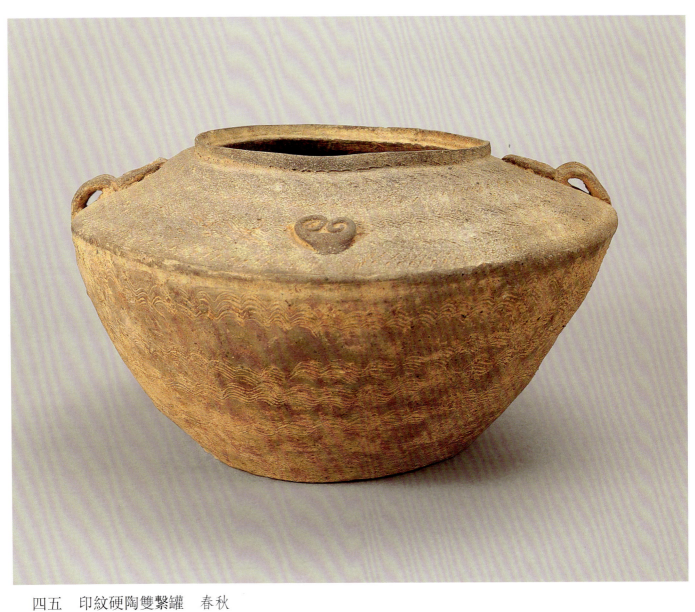

四五　印紋硬陶雙繫罐　春秋

45. Hard Pottery Jar with Stamped Design and Two Loop Handles　*Spring & Autumn Period (770 ~ 476 BC)*

四六　印紋硬陶鳥耳罐　春秋
46. Hard Pottery Jar with Stamped Design and Bird-shaped Handles　*Spring & Autumn Period (770 ~ 476 BC)*

四七　印紋硬陶罐　春秋
47.Hard Pottery Jar with Stamped Design　*Spring & Autumn Period (770 ~ 476 BC)*

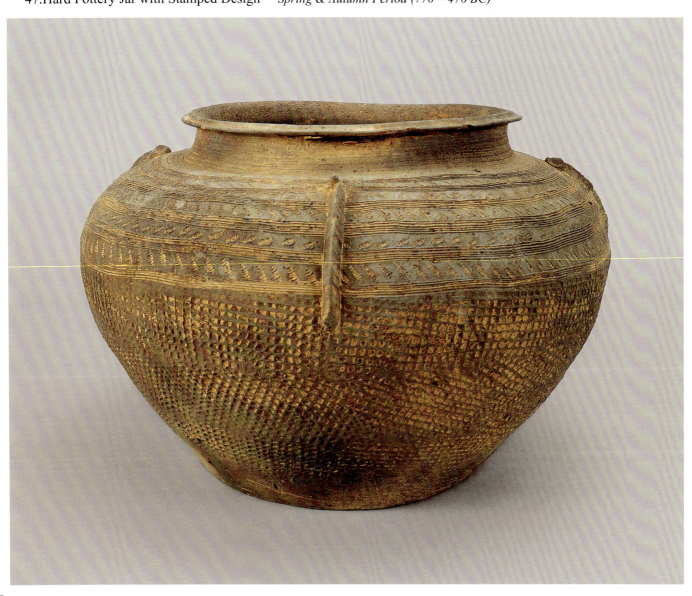

四八　印紋硬陶雙繫罐　春秋

48. Hard Pottery Jar with Stamped Design and Two Loop Handles　*Spring & Autumn Period (770 ~ 476 BC)*

四九　印紋硬陶瓿　春秋

49. Hard Pottery *Bu* (vase) with Stamped Design　*Spring & Autumn Period (770 ~ 476 BC)*

五〇　印紋硬陶四繫罐　春秋

50. Hard Pottery Jar with Stamped Design and Four Loop Handles　*Spring & Autumn Period (770 ~ 476 BC)*

五一　印紋硬陶雙耳罐　春秋

51.Two-handled Hard Pottery Jar with Stamped Design　*Spring & Autumn Period (770 ~ 476 BC)*

五二　印紋硬陶雙繫量　春秋
52. Hard Pottery *Liang* (gauge) with Stamped Design and Two Loop Handles　*Spring & Autumn Period (770 ~ 476 BC)*

五三　印紋硬陶四繫罐　春秋

53. Hard Pottery Jar with Stamped Design and Four Loop Handles　*Spring & Autumn Period (770 ~ 476 BC)*

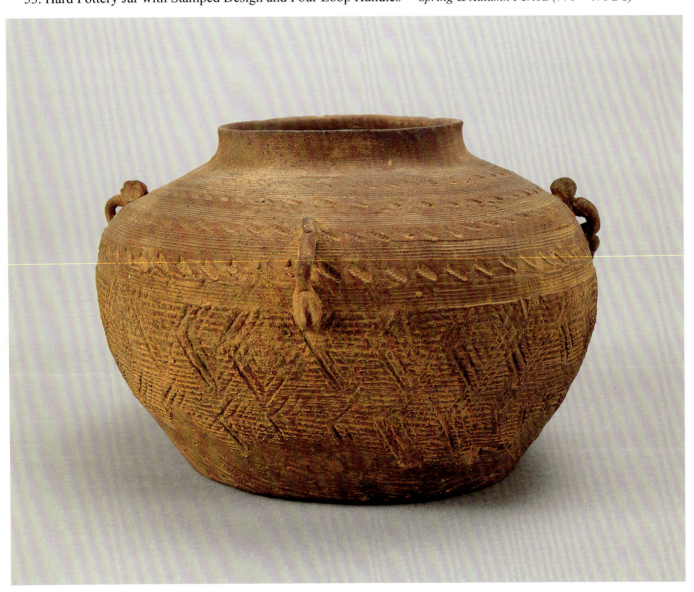

五五　印紋硬陶罐　春秋
55. Hard Pottery Jar with Stamped Design　*Spring & Autumn Period (770 ~ 476 BC)*

五六　印紋硬陶罍　春秋
56. Hard Pottery Jug with Stamped Design　*Spring & Autumn Period (770 ~ 476 BC)*

五七　印紋硬陶罐　春秋

57. Hard Pottery Jug with Stamped Design　*Spring & Autumn Period (770 ~ 476 BC)*

五八　印紋硬陶罌　春秋
58. Hard Pottery Jug with Stamped Design　*Spring & Autumn Period (770 ~ 476 BC)*

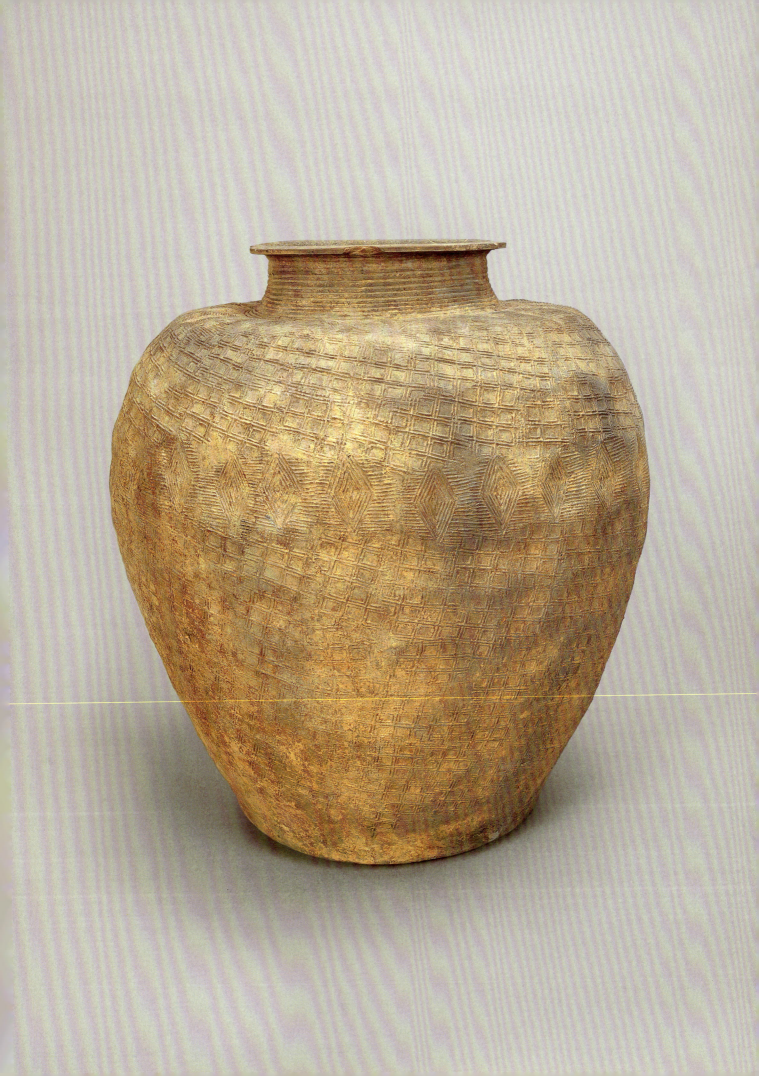

六〇　印紋硬陶雙耳筒形罐　春秋
60. Two-handled Hard Pottery Jar with Stamped Design　*Spring & Autumn Period (770 ~ 476 BC)*

五九　印紋硬陶罐　春秋
59.Hard Pottery Jug with Stamped Design　*Spring & Autumn Period (770 ~ 476 BC)*

六一　印紋硬陶罌　春秋
61. Hard Pottery Jug with Stamped Design　*Spring & Autumn Period (770 ~ 476 BC)*

六二　印紋硬陶罌　春秋
62. Hard Pottery Jug with Stamped Design　*Spring & Autumn Period (770 ~ 476 BC)*

六三　印紋硬陶雙繫罎　春秋

63. Hard Pottery Jug with Stamped Design and Two Loop Handles　*Spring & Autumn Period (770 ~ 476 BC)*

六四　印紋硬陶罐　春秋
64. Hard Pottery Jar with Stamped Design　*Spring & Autumn Period (770 ~ 476 BC)*

六六　印紋硬陶三足鼎　戰國

66. Hard Pottery Tripodal *Ding* (cooking vessel) with Stamped Design　*Warring States Period (475 ~ 221 BC)*

六五　印紋硬陶罐　春秋

65. Hard Pottery Jug with Stamped Design　*Spring & Autumn Period (770 ~ 476 BC)*

六七　印紋硬陶貫耳罐（十件）　戰國

67. Hard Pottery Jar with Stamped Design and Pierced Handles (10 Articles)　*Warring States Period (475 ~ 221 BC)*

六八　印紋硬陶倉　戰　國

68. Hard Pottery Barn with Stamped Design　*Warring States Period (475 ~ 221 BC)*

七〇　灰陶插座　戰國
70.Grey Pottery Receptacle　*Warring States Period (475 ~ 221 BC)*

六九　印紋硬陶倉　戰國
69. Hard Pottery Barn with Stamped Design　*Warring States Period (475 ~ 221 BC)*

七一　灰陶雙繫罐　戰國

71. Grey Pottery Jar with Two Loop Handles

Warring States Period (475 ~ 221 BC)

七二　印紋硬陶帶把罐（三件）　戰 國

72. Hard Pottery Jar with Stamped Design and Handle (3 Articles)　　*Warring States Period (475 ~ 221 BC)*

七三　印紋硬陶筒形罐（三件）　戰國

73. Hard Pottery Jar with Stamped Design (3 Articles)　*Warring States Period (475 ~ 221 BC)*

七四　硬陶虎子　戰國
74. Hard Pottery Chamber Pot　*Warring States Period (475 ~ 221 BC)*

七五　印紋硬陶雙繫罐　戰國
75. Hard Pottery Jar with Stamped
　　Design and Two Loop Handles
　　Warring States Period (475～221 BC)

七六　灰陶虎子　漢
76. Grey Pottery Chamber Pot　*Han (206 BC ~ 220 AD)*

七七　灰陶井　漢

77. Grey Pottery well　*Han (206 BC ~ 220 AD)*

七八　釉陶羊首虎子　東漢
78. Glazed Pottery Chamber Pot with Goat-head Spout　*Eastern Han (25 ~ 220 AD)*

七九　釉陶虎子　東漢
79. Glazed Pottery Chamber Pot　*Eastern Han (25 ~ 220 AD)*

八〇 釉陶虎子 東漢
80. Glazed Pottery Chamber Pot   *Eastern Han (25 ~ 220 AD)*

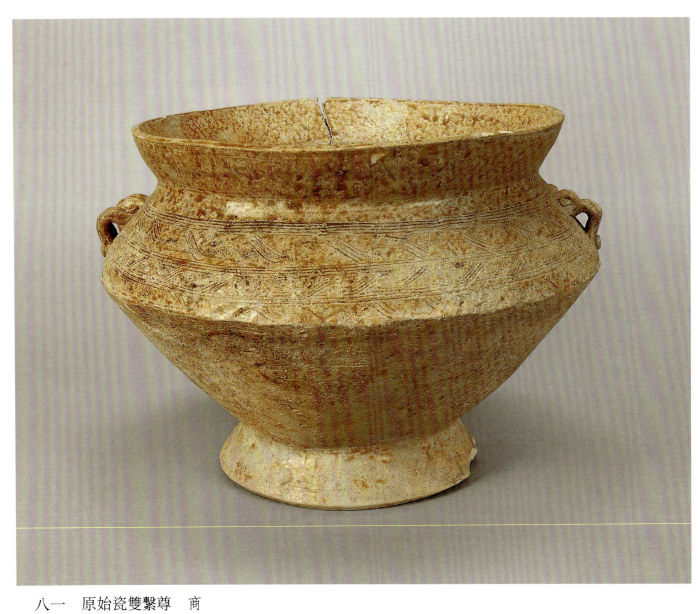

八一　原始瓷雙繫尊　商
81. Proto-porcelain *Zun* (wine vessel) with Two Loop Handles　*Shang (1600 ~ 1046 BC)*

八二　原始瓷豆　西周

82. Proto-porcelain *Dou* (stemmed bowl)　*Western Zhou (1046 ~ 771 BC)*

八三　原始瓷蓋盂　西周

83. Proto-porcelain *Yu* (broad-mouthed receptacle)

Western Zhou (1046 ~ 771 BC)

八四　原始瓷鼎　春秋早期

84. Proto-porcelain *Ding* (cooking vessel)　*Early Spring & Autumn Period　(770 ~ 677 BC)*

八五　原始瓷盂　春秋早期

85. Proto-porcelain *Yu* (broad-mouthed receptacle)　　*Early Spring & Autumn Period　(770 ~ 677 BC)*

八六　原始瓷尊　春秋
86. Proto-porcelain *Zun* (wine vessel)　*Spring & Autumn Period　(770 ~ 476 BC)*

127

八七　原始瓷雙繫罐　春秋

87. Proto-porcelain Jar with Two Loop Handles　*Spring & Autumn Period　(770 ~ 476 BC)*

八八　原始瓷鑒　春秋
88. Proto-porcelain *Jian* (vat)　*Spring & Autumn Period (770 ~ 476 BC)*

八九　原始瓷簋　春秋

89. Proto-porcelain *Gui* (food container)　*Spring & Autumn Period (770 ~ 476 BC)*

九〇　原始瓷壶　春秋
90. Proto-porcelain Ewer　*Spring & Autumn Period (770 ~476 BC)*

九一 原始瓷罐 春秋
91. Proto-porcelain Jar   *Spring & Autumn Period (770 ~ 476 BC)*

九二　原始瓷盤　戰國

92. Proto-porcelain Plate　*Warring States Period (475 ~ 221 BC)*

九三　原始瓷薰　戰國

93. Proto-porcelain Censer　*Warring States Period (475～221 BC)*

134

九五　原始瓷烤爐　戰國

95. Proto-porcelain Roaster　*Warring States Period (475 ~ 221 BC)*

九六　原始瓷雙繫大罐　戰國
96. Proto-porcelain Jar with Two Loop Handles　*Warring States Period (475 ~ 221 BC)*

九七　原始瓷雙繫罐　戰國

97. Proto-porcelain Jar with Two Loop Handles　*Warring States Period (475 ~ 221 BC)*

九八　原始瓷瓿　戰國
98. Proto-porcelain *Bu* (vase)　*Warring States Period (475～221 BC)*

139

九九　原始瓷洗　戰國

99. Proto-porcelain *Xi* (basin-shaped vessel for washing)　*Warring States Period (475 ~ 221 BC)*

一〇〇　原始瓷雙繫罐　戰 國

100. Proto-porcelain Jar with Two Loop Handles　*Warring States Period (475 ~ 221 BC)*

一〇一　原始瓷釉下彩鈴　戰國

101. Proto-porcelain *Ling* (similar to bell but much smaller) in Underglaze Colours

　　Warring States Period (475 ~ 221 BC)

一〇二　原始瓷錞于　戰國

102. Proto-porcelain *Chun Yu* (military musical instrument)　　*Warring States Period (475 ~ 221 BC)*

144

一〇四　原始瓷龍　戰國
104. Proto-porcelain Dragon　*Warring States Period (475 ~ 221 BC)*

一〇三　原始瓷句鑼　戰國
103. Proto-porcelain *Gou Diao* (musical instrument used at sacrificial ceremonies or feasts)
　　Warring States Period (475 ~ 221 BC)

一〇五　原始瓷壺　戰國

105. Proto-porcelain Ewer　*Warring States Period (475 ~ 221 BC)*

一〇六　原始瓷壺　戰國
106. Proto-porcelain Ewer　　*Warring States Period (475 ~ 221 BC)*

一〇七　原始瓷雙耳瓿　戰國

107. Two-handled Proto-porcelain *Bu* (vase)　　*Warring States Period (475 ~ 221 BC)*

108. Proto-porcelain *Yi* (elliptical ewer for washing)　*Warring States Period (475 ~ 221 BC)*

一〇九　原始瓷提梁盉　戰 國

109. Loop-handled Proto-porcelain *He* (tripodal container for holding wine)　　*Warring States Period (475 ~ 221 BC)*

一一〇　原始瓷雙繫罐　戰國

110. Proto-porcelain Jar with Two Loop Handles　*Warring States Period (475 ~ 221 BC)*

一一一　原始瓷蓋碗（六件）　戰國

111. Covered Proto-porcelain Bowl (6 Articles)　*Warring States Period (475 ~ 221 BC)*

一一三　原始瓷匜　戰國

113. Proto-porcelain *Yi* (elliptical ewer for washing)　　*Warring States Period (475 ~ 221 BC)*

一一四　原始瓷直口小罐（兩件）　戰國
114. Proto-porcelain Pots (2 Articles)　*Warring States Period (475 ~ 221 BC)*

一一五　原始瓷鼎　戰國

115. Proto-porcelain *Ding* (cooking vessel)　*Warring States Period (475 ~ 221 BC)*

一一六　原始瓷獸面鼎　戰國

116. Proto-porcelain *Ding* (cooking vessel) with Beast Mask Pattern　　*Warring States Period (475 ~ 221 BC)*

一一七 原始瓷鼎 戰國

117. Proto-porcelain *Ding* (cooking vessel)　　*Warring States Period (475 ~ 221 BC)*

一一八　原始瓷鼎　戰國

118. Proto-porcelain *Ding* (cooking vessel)　*Warring States Period (475 ~ 221 BC)*

一一九　原始瓷鼎　戰國

119. Proto-porcelain *Ding* (cooking vessel)　*Warring States Period (475～221 BC)*

一二一　原始瓷鼎　戰國

121. Proto-porcelain *Ding* (cooking vessel)　*Warring States Period (475 ~ 221 BC)*

一二二　原始瓷鼎　戰國

122. Proto-porcelain *Ding* (cooking vessel)　*Warring States Period (475 ~ 221 BC)*

一二四　原始瓷虎子　戰 國
124. Proto-porcelain Chamber Pot　*Warring States Period (475 ~ 221 BC)*

一二三　原始瓷甗　戰國
123. Proto-porcelain *Yan* (cooking vessel)　*Warring States Period (475 ~ 221 BC)*

一二五　原始瓷虎子　戰國

125. Proto-porcelain Chamber Pot　*Warring States Period (475 ~ 221 BC)*

一二六　原始瓷虎子　戰國

126. Proto-porcelain Chamber Pot　*Warring States Period (475 ~ 221 BC)*

一二七　原始瓷豆（兩件）　戰國

127. Proto-porcelain *Dou* (stemmed bowl) (2 Articles)　*Warring States Period (475 ~ 221 BC)*

一二八　原始瓷帶流罐　戰國
128. Proto-porcelain Jar with Spout　*Warring States Period (475 ~ 221 BC)*

一二九　原始瓷雙繫筒形罐（兩件）　戰 國

129. Proto-porcelain Jar with Two Loop Handles (2 Articles)　*Warring States Period (475 ~ 221 BC)*

一三〇　原始瓷熏爐　戰國至西漢
130. Proto-porcelain Censer　*Warring States Period ~ Western Han (475BC ~ 8 AD)*

一三一　原始瓷瓿　西漢

131. Proto-porcelain *Bu* (vase)　*Western Han (206 BC ~ 8 AD)*

一三二　原始瓷熏爐　西漢
132. Proto-porcelain Censer　*Western Han (206 BC ~ 8 AD)*

一三三　原始瓷熏爐　漢

133. Proto-porcelain Censer　*Han (206 BC ~ 220 AD)*

一三四　原始瓷匜　漢
134. Proto-porcelain *Yi* (elliptical ewer for washing)　*Han (206 BC ~ 220 AD)*

一三五　原始瓷五管瓶　漢

135. Proto-porcelain Vase with Five Spouts　*Han (206 BC ~ 220 AD)*

一三六　原始瓷鼎　漢
136. Proto-porcelain *Ding* (cooking vessel)　*Han (206 BC ~ 220 AD)*

一三七　原始瓷長頸瓶　漢

137. Proto-porcelain Flask　*Han (206 BC ~ 220 AD)*

一三八　原始瓷井與吊桶　東漢
138. Proto-porcelain Well and Bucket　*Eastern Han (25 ~ 220 AD)*

179

一三九　原始瓷虎子　東漢

139. Proto-porcelain Chamber Pot　*Eastern Han (25 ~ 220 AD)*

一四〇　褐釉熏爐　東漢
140. Brown-glazed Censer　*Eastern Han (25 ~ 220 AD)*

一四一　青瓷鍾　東漢
141. Celadon *Zhong* (bell)　*Eastern Han (25 ~ 220 AD)*

一四二　醬釉鍾　東漢
142. Brown-glazed *Zhong* (bell)　*Eastern Han (25 ~ 220 AD)*

一四三　青瓷五管瓶　東漢

143. Celadon Vase with Five Spouts　*Eastern Han (25 ~ 220 AD)*

一四四　黑釉五管瓶　東漢

144. Black-glazed Vase with Five Spouts　*Eastern Han (25 ~ 220 AD)*

一四五　黑釉酒具　東漢

145. Black-glazed Wine Vessel　*Eastern Han (25 ~ 220 AD)*

一四六　黑釉盤口壺　東漢
146. Black-glazed Ewer with a Dish-shaped Mouth　*Eastern Han (25 ~ 220 AD)*

一四七　越窰青瓷雙繫罐　東漢

147. Celadon Jar with Two Loop Handles from the *Yue* Kiln　*Eastern Han (25 ~ 220 AD)*

一四八　越窰青瓷堆塑罐　三國吳

148. Celadon Jar with Embossed Decoration (burial object) from the *Yue* Kiln

Wu, the Three Kingdoms (222 ~ 280 AD)

一四九　越窰青瓷虎子　三國吳

149. Celadon Chamber Pot from the *Yue* Kiln　*Wu, the Three Kingdoms (222～280 AD)*

一五〇　越窯青瓷洗　三國吳

150. Celadon *Xi* (basin-shaped vessel for washing) from the *Yue* Kiln　*Wu, the Three Kingdoms (222 ~ 280 AD)*

一五一　褐釉蛙形盉　三國吳

151. Brown-glazed Frog-shaped *Yu* (broad-mouthed receptacle)　*Wu, the Three Kingdoms (222 ~ 280 AD)*

一五二　越窰青瓷虎子　三國吳

152. Celadon Chamber Pot from the *Yue* Kiln　*Wu, the Three Kingdoms (222 ~ 280 AD)*

一五三　越窑青瓷武士俑　西晋

153. Celadon Warrior Figurine from the *Yue* Kiln　*Western Jin (265 ~ 316 AD)*

一五五　越窯青瓷男俑　西晉

155. Celadon Man Figurine from the *Yue* Kiln　*Western Jin (265 ~ 316 AD)*

一五七　越窯青瓷女俑　西晉

157. Celadon Maid of Honour Figurine from the *Yue* Kiln　*Western Jin (265～316 AD)*

一五八　越窑青瓷女俑　西晋

158. Celadon Maid of Honour Figurine from the *Yue* Kiln　*Western Jin (265 ~ 316 AD)*

一五九　越窰青瓷男女俑（四件）　西晉
159. Celadon Figurines from the *Yue* Kiln (4 Articles)　*Western Jin (265 ~ 316 AD)*

一六〇　越窑青瓷樽　西晋
160. Celadon *Zun* (wine vessel) from the *Yue* Kiln　*Western Jin (265 ~ 316 AD)*

一六一　越窑青瓷狮形插座　西晋
161. Lion-shaped Celadon Receptacle from the *Yue* Kiln　*Western Jin (265 ~ 316 AD)*

一六二　越窯青瓷虎頭罐　西晉

162. Celadon Jar with Tiger-head Decoration from the *Yue* Kiln　*Western Jin (265～316 AD)*

一六三　越窯青瓷虎子　西晉

163. Celadon Chamber Pot from the *Yue* Kiln　*Western Jin (265 ~ 316 AD)*

一六四　越窑青瓷虎子　西晋

164. Celadon Chamber Pot from the *Yue* Kiln　*Western Jin (265 ~ 316 AD)*

一六五　越窰青瓷盤口壺　西晋

165. Dish-mouthed Celadon Ewer from the *Yue* Kiln　*Western Jin (265 ~ 316 AD)*

一六六　越窰青瓷雙繫罐　西晉
166.Celadon Jar with Two Loop Handles from the *Yue* Kiln　*Western Jin (265～316 AD)*

一六七　越窑青瓷盆　西晋
167. Celadon *Pen* (water basin) from the *Yue* Kiln　*Western Jin (265 ~ 316 AD)*

208

一六八　越窰青瓷四繫罐　西晉
168. Celadon Jar with Four Loop Handles from the *Yue* Kiln　*Western Jin (265～316 AD)*

一六九　越窯青瓷貝紋四繫罐　西晉

169. Celadon Jar with Four Loop Handles and Cowrie Pattern from the *Yue* Kiln　　*Western Jin (265 ~ 316 AD)*

一七一　越窰青瓷四繫罐　西晉

171. Celadon Jar with Four Loop Handles from the *Yue* Kiln　*Western Jin (265 ~ 316 AD)*

一七二　越窰青瓷盤口壺　西晉
172. Dish-mouthed Celadon Ewer from the *Yue* Kiln　*Western Jin (265 ~ 316 AD)*

一七三　越窑青瓷盘口壶　西晋

173. Dish-mouthed Celadon Ewer from the *Yue* Kiln　*Western Jin (265 ~ 316 AD)*

一七四　越窑青瓷双系扁壶　西晋

174. Celadon Flask with Two Loop Handles from the *Yue* Kiln　*Western Jin (265 ~ 316 AD)*

215

一七五　越窑青瓷熏炉　西晋

175. Celadon Censer from the *Yue* Kiln　*Western Jin (265 ~ 316 AD)*

一七六　越窯青瓷手爐　西晉
176. Celadon Hand Warmer from the *Yue* Kiln　*Western Jin (265～316 AD)*

一七七　越窯青瓷硯　西晉

177.Celadon Inkstone from the *Yue* Kiln　*Western Jin (265～316 AD)*

一七八　越窯青瓷三足硯　西晉
178. Celadon Tripodal Inkstone from the *Yue* Kiln　*Western Jin (265 ~ 316 AD)*

一七九　越窰青瓷三足硯　西晉
179. Celadon Tripodal Inkstone from the *Yue* Kiln　*Western Jin (265 ~ 316 AD)*

一八〇　越窯青瓷盤　西晉
180. Celadon Plate from the *Yue* Kiln　*Western Jin (265 ~ 316 AD)*

一八一　越窑青瓷竈　西晉

181. Celadon Cooking Stove from the *Yue* Kiln　*Western Jin (265～316 AD)*

一八二　越窯青瓷竈　西晉

182. Celadon Cooking Stove from the *Yue* Kiln　*Western Jin (265 ~ 316 AD)*

一八三　越窰青瓷豬圈　西晉

183.Celadon Pigsty from the *Yue* Kiln　*Western Jin (265 ~ 316 AD)*

一八四　越窰青瓷豬圈　西晉
184. Celadon Pigsty from the *Yue* Kiln　*Western Jin (265 ~ 316 AD)*

一八五　越窰青瓷豬圈與茅廁　西晉

185. Celadon Pigsty and Toilet from the *Yue* Kiln　*Western Jin (265～316 AD)*

一八六　越窑青瓷狗圈　西晋
186. Celadon Doghouse from the *Yue* Kiln　*Western Jin (265 ~ 316 AD)*

一八七　越窑青瓷羊　西晋

187. Celadon Goat from the *Yue* Kiln　*Western Jin (265 ~ 316 AD)*

一八八　越窑青瓷鹅（两件）　西晋
188. Celadon Goose from the *Yue* Kiln　*Western Jin (265～316 AD)*

一八九　越窰青瓷竹筒形雞籠　西晉

189. Celadon Chick Coop from the *Yue* Kiln　*Western Jin (265 ~ 316 AD)*

一九〇　越窑青瓷井　西晋
190. Celadon Well from the *Yue* Kiln　*Western Jin (265～316 AD)*

一九二　越窯青瓷槅　西晉

192. Celadon *Ge* (food container) from the *Yue* Kiln　*Western Jin (265 ~ 316 AD)*

一九一　越窯青瓷穿帶扁壺　西晉

191. Celadon Flask with Tubular Handles from the *Yue* Kiln　*Western Jin (265 ~ 316 AD)*

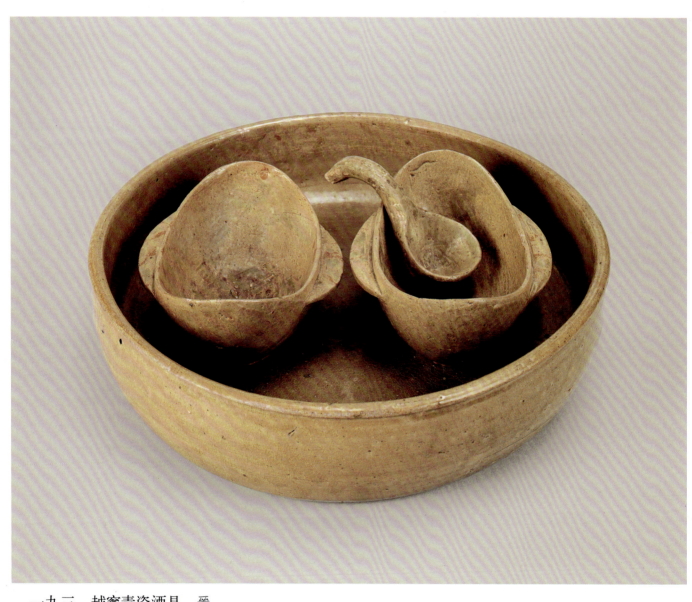

一九三　越窯青瓷酒具　晉

193. Celadon Wine Vessel from the *Yue* Kiln　*Jin (265 ~ 420 AD)*

一九四　越窑青瓷洗　晋

194. Celadon *Xi* (basin-shaped vessel for washing) from the *Yue* Kiln　*Jin (265~420 AD)*

一九五　越窰青瓷榻　東晉咸和八年
195. Celadon *Ge* (food container) from
the *Yue* Kiln　*The 8th Year of
XianHe, Eastern Jin (333 AD)*

一九六　越窯青瓷洗
東晉咸和八年

196. Celadon *Xi* (basin-shaped vessel
for washing) from the *Yue* Kiln
*The 8th Year of XianHe, Eastern
Jin (333 AD)*

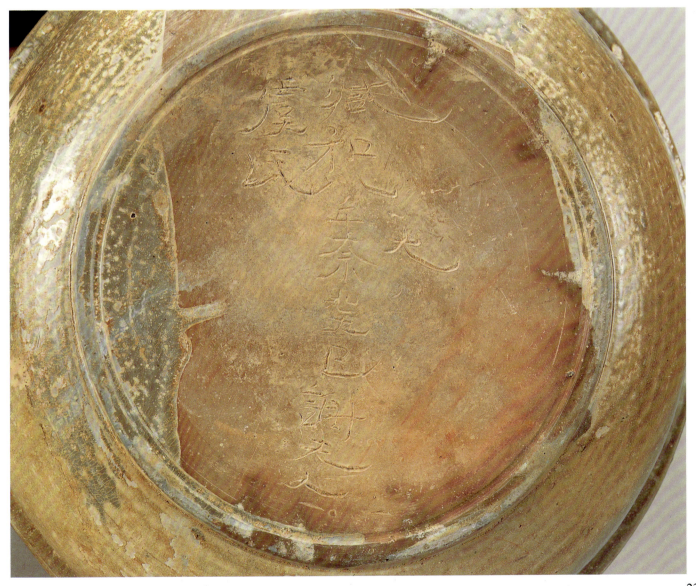

一九七　越窰青瓷槅　東晉

197. Celadon *Ge* (food container) from the *Yue* Kiln　*Eastern Jin (317～420 AD)*

一九八　越窯青瓷蛙形尊　東晉

198. Frog-shaped Celadon *Zun* (wine vessel) from the *Yue* Kiln　*Eastern Jin (317 ~ 420 AD)*

一九九　越窯青瓷雞首壺　東晉

199. Celadon Ewer with Chicken Spout from the *Yue* Kiln　*Eastern Jin (317 ~ 420 AD)*

二〇〇　越窯青瓷雞首壺　東晉
200. Celadon Ewer with Chicken Spout from the *Yue* Kiln　*Eastern Jin (317 ~ 420 AD)*

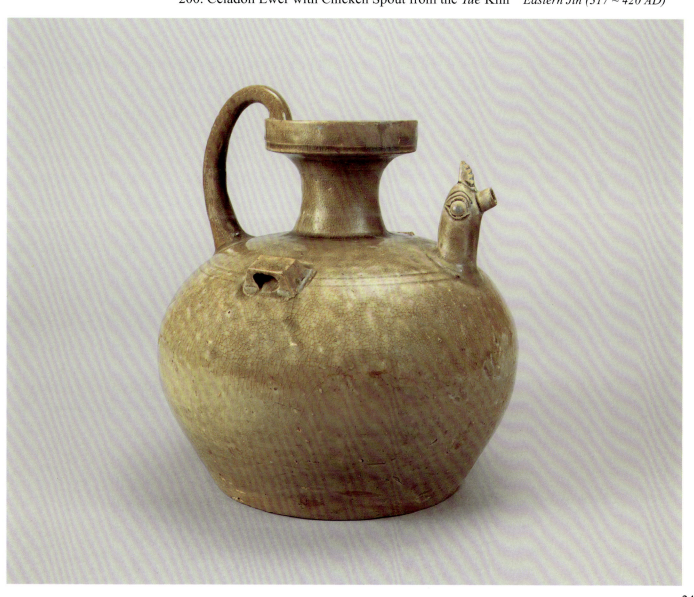

二〇一　甌窰青瓷雞首壺　東晉

201. Celadon Ewer with Chicken Spout from the *Ou* Kiln　*Eastern Jin (317～420 AD)*

二〇二　青瓷龍柄雞首壺　東晉
202. Celadon Ewer with Chicken Spout and Dragon Handle　*Eastern Jin (317~420 AD)*

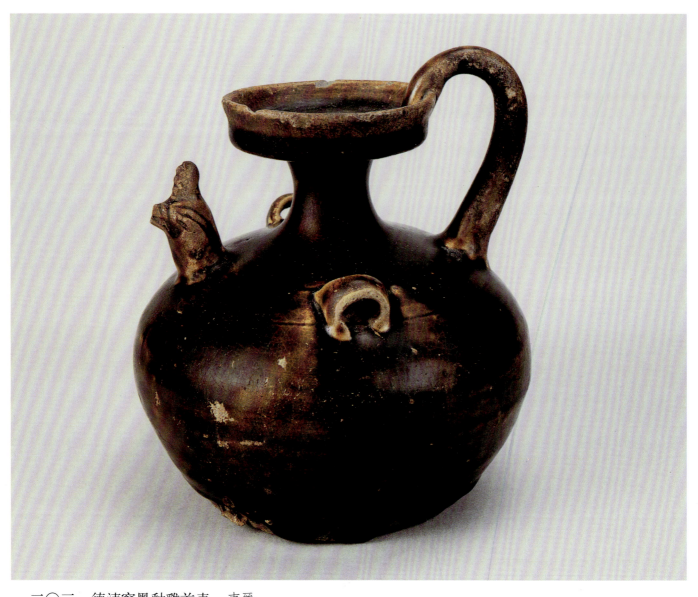

二〇三　德清窯黑釉雞首壺　東晉

203. Black-glazed Ewer with Chicken Spout from the *Deqing* Kiln　*Eastern Jin (317 ~ 420 AD)*

二〇四　越窯青瓷雞首壺　東晉

204. Celadon Ewer with Chicken Spout from the *Yue* Kiln　*Eastern Jin (317 ~ 420 AD)*

二〇五　越窰青瓷八繫盤口壺　東晉

205. Dish-mouthed Celadon Ewer with Eight Loop Handles from the *Yue* Kiln　*Eastern Jin (317 ~ 420 AD)*

二〇六　越窯青瓷雙繫筒形罐　東晉
206. Celadon Jar with Two Loop Handles from the *Yue* Kiln　*Eastern Jin (317 ~ 420 AD)*

二〇七　越窑青瓷虎子　東晉

207. Celadon Chamber Pot from the *Yue* Kiln　*Eastern Jin (317 ~ 420 AD)*

二〇八　越窯青瓷虎子　東晉
208. Celadon Chamber Pot from the *Yue* Kiln　*Eastern Jin (317 ~ 420 AD)*

二〇九　越窑青瓷唾壶　東晉
209. Celadon Spittoon from the *Yue* Kiln　*Eastern Jin (317 ~ 420 AD)*

二一二　越窯褐斑點彩罐　東晉
212. Jar with Brown Stippling Decoration from the *Yue* Kiln　*Eastern Jin (317 ~ 420 AD)*

二一一　越窯青瓷褐彩六繫盤口壺　東晉
211. Dish-mouthed Celadon Ewer with Six Loop Handles and Brown Decorations from the *Yue* Kiln

    Eastern Jin (317 ~ 420 AD)

二一三　越窯青瓷簋　東晉

213. Celadon *Gui* (food container)
from the *Yue* Kiln
Eastern Jin (317 ~ 420 AD)

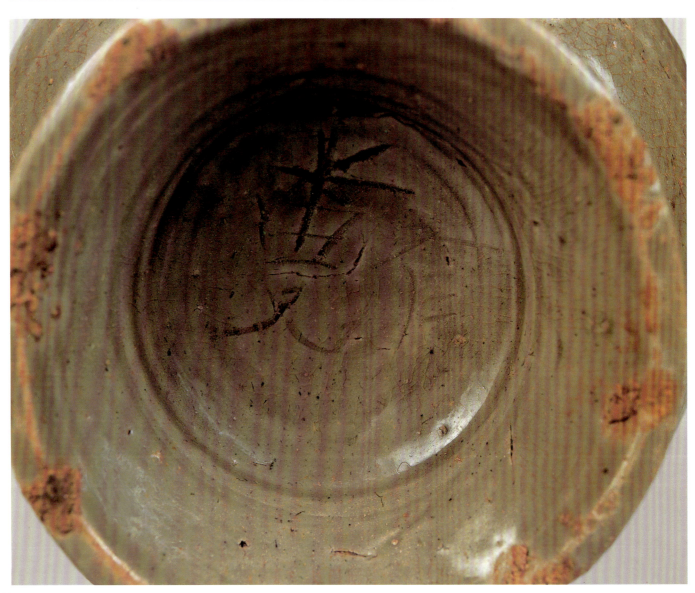

二一四　青瓷虎子　南朝
214. Celadon Chamber Pot　*Southern Dynasties (420 ~ 589 AD)*

二一五 青瓷虎子 南朝

215. Celadon Chamber Pot *Southern Dynasties (420 ~ 589 AD)*

二一六　青瓷二俑竈
南朝
216. Celadon Cooking Stove
and Two Figurines
Southern Dynasties
(420～589AD)

257

二一七　青瓷二俑竈　南朝
217. Celadon Cooking Stove and
　　 Two Figurines　*Southern*
　　 Dynasties (420 ~ 589 AD)

二一八　青瓷蓮紋盤　南朝

218. Celadon Plate with Lotus Pattern　*Southern Dynasties (420 ~ 589 AD)*

二一九　越窑青瓷盘龙罂　唐

219. Celadon *Ying* (round jar with a small opening) with Coiled Dragon Design from the *Yue* Kiln　　*Tang (618 ~ 907 AD)*

220.Celadon *Ying* (round jar with a small opening) with Coiled Dragon Design from the *Yue* Kiln　　*Tang (618 ~ 907 AD)*

二二一　越窰青瓷錢氏墓地界碑　唐貞元十八年

221. Celadon Boundary Tablet of the *Qian's* Graveyard from the *Yue* Kiln

The 18th Year of ZhenYuan ,Tang Dynasty (802 AD)

二二二　越窯青瓷墓誌銘　唐大和六年
222. Celadon Epitaph from the *Yue* Kiln
The 6th Year of DaHe, Tang Dynasty (832 AD)

二二三　越窑青瓷钵　唐

223. Celadon *Bo* (small basin-shaped container) from the *Yue* Kiln　*Tang (618 ~ 907 AD)*

二二四　越窯青瓷帶流罐　唐
224. Celadon Jar with Spout from the *Yue* Kiln　*Tang (618 ~ 907 AD)*

二二五　越窰青瓷墓誌罐　唐

225. Celadon Jar with Epitaph from the *Yue* Kiln　*Tang (618 ~ 907 AD)*

226. Two-handled Celadon Jar from the *Yue* Kiln   *Tang (618 ~ 907 AD)*

二二七 越窑青瓷注子 唐

227. Celadon Ewer from the *Yue* Kiln *Tang (618 ~ 907 AD)*

二二八　越窑青瓷注子　唐

228. Celadon Ewer from the *Yue* Kiln　*Tang (618 ~ 907 AD)*

二二九　青瓷圈足硯　唐

229.Celadon Inkstone with Ring Foot　*Tang (618～907 AD)*

二三〇　越窯青瓷雙繫罌　唐

230. Celadon *Ying* (round jar with a small opening) with Two Loop Handles from the *Yue* Kiln　*Tang (618～907 AD)*

二三一　青瓷粉盒　唐

231. Celadon Compact　*Tang (618 ~ 907 AD)*

二三二　青瓷碗　唐
232. Celadon Bowl　*Tang (618 ~ 907 AD)*

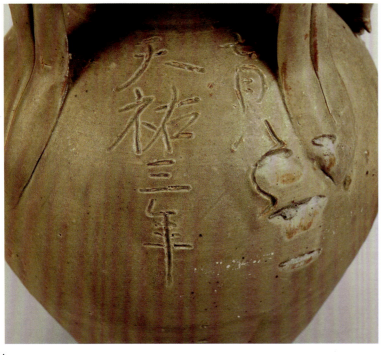

二三三　越窰青瓷盤龍罍　唐天佑三年

233. Celadon *Ying* (round jar with a small opening) with Coiled Dragon Design from the *Yue* Kiln

The 3rd Year of TianYou, Tang Dynasty (906 AD)

二三四　越窑青瓷粉盒　五代

234. Celadon Compact from the *Yue* Kiln　*Five Dynasties (907 ~ 960 AD)*

二三五　越窰青瓷粉盒　北宋
235. Celadon Compact from the *Yue*
Kiln
Northern Song (960～1127AD)

二三六　越窰青瓷罐　北宋
236. Celadon Jar from the *Yue* Kiln
Northern Song (960～1127 AD)

二三七　越窯青瓷鳥形哨　北宋

237. Bird-shaped Celadon Whistle from
the *Yue* Kiln

Northern Song (960 ~ 1127 AD)

圖 版 説 明

NOTES ON THE PLATES

圖 版 説 明

陶 器 篇

一 黑陶豆
跨湖橋文化（距今約 8000～7000 年）
殘高 10.4、口徑 18.3 厘米

敞口，圓唇，淺腹。腹底呈一週突稜。高圈足，圈足上部飾凹凸相間的弦紋。內外兩面漆黑光亮。

二 黑陶豆
跨湖橋文化（距今約 8000～7000 年）
高 7、口徑 14 厘米

敞口，圓唇，深腹。圈足低矮外撇。下腹上下緣各有一週較尖銳的凸稜，下部凸稜帶鋸齒。內外兩面漆黑光亮，造型較爲完整，顯示了當時製陶工藝的水平。

三 黑陶弦紋雙耳罐
跨湖橋文化（距今約 8000～7000 年）
口徑 16.6 厘米

尖圓唇，口微斂，斜領，領部有七道平行凹弦紋。折頸處爲一圈突脊，脊處起耳連肩部，折肩深腹。夾炭陶，外壁漆黑光亮。內壁除了口沿，均顯不平。肩部略凸，接痕明顯。此器殘甚，未能修復，不過仍然顯示出慢輪製器的特徵。

四 紅衣灰陶雙耳折腹罐
跨湖橋文化（距今約 8000～7000 年）
高 13、口徑 20.8 厘米

直口，尖圓唇，折頸，折肩，扁腹，圜底。肩部以上施紅衣，肩以下爲灰褐色，有向心分佈的黑斑。頸上突稜呈鋸齒狀。耳的正面有一"田"字形彩繪紋飾。

五 紅衣黑裏陶缽
跨湖橋文化（距今約 8000～7000 年）
高 9.8、口徑 16.7 厘米

口微敞，方唇中凹，深腹，圜底。外施紅彩，內壁漆黑光亮。

六 紅衣灰陶豆
跨湖橋文化（距今約 8000～7000 年）
高 14.9、口徑 17.5、足徑 13.8 厘米

斂口，尖圓唇，腹微折，高柄圈足，足底呈倒盤口。上腹有三道規則弦紋。圈足部位的放射綫以雙孔爲中心展開。器身內外殘留紅衣。

七 黑陶雙耳罐
跨湖橋文化（距今約 8000～7000 年）
高 13.6、口徑 12.4 厘米

尖圓唇，束頸，窄斜肩，深弧腹，圓角小平底。夾炭陶，器身多黑，頸肩部殘留紅衣。器內不平，積有雜質。

八 太陽紋彩陶片
跨湖橋文化（距今約 8000～7000 年）
長 3.8、寬 3 厘米

彩色陶衣上面以白色同心圓爲中心，環其週圍繪白色放射紋。一般見於罐類器的肩、腹以及領沿部位。

九 灰陶支座
跨湖橋文化（距今約 8000～7000 年）
高 6.5、底 5.2 × 4.3 厘米

器爲六面體。頂部呈方形斜面，弧背內斜，底呈四方形平面。一側面有一鏤孔。局部有火紅色痕。

一〇　灰陶裹手

跨湖橋文化（距今約 8000～7000 年）

高 8.3～6.2 厘米

裹手是一種製陶的工具。每件器物有圓柱形柄。底爲弧形面，呈蘑菇狀。

一一　印紋硬陶提梁盉

商（公元前 1600～前 1046 年）

高 19.2、流口徑 5.4 厘米

敞口，縮頸，廣圓肩，略鼓腹，下腹速收，圈底內凹。拱形蓋上飾橋形提梁。流爲敞口，圓唇，弧粗頸。肩部起稜，稜下器身遍飾編織紋。

一二　印紋硬陶罐

商（公元前 1600～前 1046 年）

高 17.2、口徑 20.5 厘米

敞口，方唇，縮頸，下垂腹，圈底。頸以下飾斜方格紋。

一三　印紋硬陶單柄壺

商（公元前 1600～前 1046 年）

高 12、口徑 9.6 × 8.5 厘米

敞口，直頸，平肩下折，下垂鼓腹，圈底。口部一側捏塑成扁弧形流狀。頸部飾以多道弦紋，肩以下器身滿飾編織紋，器身一側寬帶狀耳形鋬柄上也飾有多道弦紋。

一四　硬陶雙耳尊

商（公元前 1600～前 1046 年）

高 22.3、口徑 28、底徑 18 厘米

敞口，寬沿略外捲，直頸，肩斜下折，下腹斜收，平底。頸部飾以多道弦紋，

肩部以弦紋夾編織紋爲主，兩側有 "S" 形彎曲的蛇形耳飾。

一五　印紋硬陶雙耳罐

商（公元前 1600～前 1046 年）

高 8.8、口徑 10.3 厘米

敞口，短粗頸，折肩，深腹，圈底。寬帶狀耳呈彎曲形，從口沿連至肩部。頸肩部有多道弦紋，腰腹部以下拍印網格紋。

一六　印紋硬陶罐

商晚期至西周早期

（公元前 1147～前 977 年）

高 20.5、口徑 17.2 厘米

略敞口，方唇，縮頸，溜肩，鼓腹，圈底內凹。口沿以下飾網狀紋飾，肩腰部有三條粗弦紋。

一七　印紋硬陶尊

西周（公元前 1046～前 771 年）

高 15.2、口徑 14.4、底徑 9.3 厘米

敞口，厚唇，縮頸，豐肩，腹斜收，外底平微內凹。口沿上有多道弦紋，肩部飾一對橋形繫，起稜處以下滿飾編織紋。

一八　印紋硬陶罐

西周（公元前 1046～前 771 年）

高 7.3、口徑 10.2、底徑 10 厘米

敞口，縮頸，鼓腹，平底。灰黑色胎。頸部飾若干弦紋。肩腹部以雲雷紋作主題裝飾，渾厚而凝重。

一九　印紋硬陶罐

西周（公元前 1046～前 771 年）

高 22.9、口徑 15、底徑 18 厘米

敞口，短頸，聳肩，弧腹，平底。灰胎。肩飾雲雷紋，腹部拍印回紋。

二〇　印紋硬陶罍

西周（公元前 1046～前 771 年）

高 23.6、口徑 13.3、底徑 13 厘米

敞口，短頸，豐肩，鼓腹，平底。褐色胎體。肩部內側飾回紋，外側爲竊曲紋，腹部以下又拍印回紋。其裝飾紋樣有明顯的仿青銅器特徵。

二一　印紋硬陶罍

西周（公元前 1046～前 771 年）

高 22.4、口徑 13.2 厘米

敞口，豐肩，鼓腹，寰底。黃褐色胎體。頸部飾有弦紋若干，通體拍飾回紋。器型敦實古樸。

二二　印紋硬陶罍

西周（公元前 1046～前 771 年）

高 33.5、口徑 17.5、底徑 19.5 厘米

敞口，豐肩，鼓腹，平底。胎色灰褐。通體是三道曲折紋與三道回紋相間。紋飾繁密，造型古樸。

二三　印紋硬陶甕

西周（公元前 1046～前 771 年）

高 55.4、口徑 27.2、底徑 32 厘米

撇口，短頸，溜肩，弧腹，平底。胎體深褐。通體相間拍印四道曲折紋與四道回紋。此器紋飾繁密，器型高大，爲西周印紋硬陶甕所少見。在蕭山博物館的藏品中，與此甕同樣的有兩件。

二四　印紋硬陶三繫罐

西周（公元前 1046～前 771 年）

高 39.2、口徑 22.3、底徑 19.6 厘米

敞口，斜肩，弧腹，平底。罐身置三條出脊，出脊的頂部皆置拱背形獸，形成三個環狀繫。褐色胎。罐身上部拍飾小方格填條紋，下部爲大斜方格填條紋。

二五　印紋硬陶罐

西周（公元前 1046～前 771 年）

高 9、口徑 13.5、底徑 14.2 厘米

敞口，溜肩，斜腹，平底。胎色深灰，局部發黑。頸肩部有若干弦紋。腹部爲曲折狀的箭羽紋與勾連紋。其紋帶有明顯的青銅器裝飾風格。

二六　印紋硬陶罐

西周（公元前 1046～前 771 年）

高 14.6、口徑 16.9、底徑 18.7 厘米

撇口，聳肩，斜腹，平底。灰胎。腹部中間飾一道雲雷紋，上下拍印回紋。

二七　印紋硬陶雙繫罐

西周（公元前 1046～前 771 年）

高 24.6、口徑 23、底徑 21.3 厘米

撇口，短頸，溜肩，鼓腹，平底。深褐色胎體。兩側置環形雙繫，週貼四條抽象形龍出脊。頸部飾弦紋若干條，肩與下腹部拍印回紋，中部拍飾曲折紋。

二八　印紋硬陶獸耳罐

西周（公元前 1046～前 771 年）

高 25.2、口徑 17.9、底徑 18.6 厘米

折口，短頸，溜肩，弧腹，平底。肩部兩側置獸形耳，形象非常生動。深灰色胎。通體拍飾菱形條紋與回紋。此器紋飾繁密，造型端莊。

二九　印紋硬陶雙耳罐

西周（公元前 1046～前 771 年）

高 31.9、口徑 9、底徑 20.5 厘米

小口，溜肩，弧腹，平底。置四條出脊。其中兩條對稱的脊上有兩個拱背獸形物，作爲雙繫，將藝術性與實用功能完美結合，設計巧妙。胎體深灰。口沿爲弦紋，通體佈滿紋飾，上部爲曲折紋，下

部飾回紋。

三〇　印紋硬陶獸耳罐

西周（公元前 1046～前 771 年）

高 39、口徑 20.5、底徑 21.2 厘米

敞口，短頸，聳肩，弧腹，平底。置四條出脊。兩條出脊上部置拱背形獸，作爲雙繫。另兩條頂部爲圓環。胎體灰中帶黑。

三一　印紋硬陶罐

春秋（公元前 770～前 476 年）

高 11.1、口徑 13.3、底徑 15.4 厘米

撇口，短頸，聳肩，鼓腹，平底。上部飾雲雷紋，下部拍印回紋。

三二　印紋硬陶雙耳壺

春秋（公元前 770～前 476 年）

高 19.6、口徑 12.7、底徑 12.7 厘米

敞口，弧頸，溜肩，鼓腹，平底。左右置環形雙耳。胎體灰中帶褐。通體飾編織紋。形似魚簍，造型別致。

三三　印紋硬陶雙繫罐

春秋（公元前 770～前 476 年）。

高 24、口徑 13、底徑 11 厘米

矮口，聳肩，鼓腹，平底。肩腹部刻畫 "3" 形的曲折紋，肩兩側貼 "S" 紋，下腹部飾編織紋。

三四　印紋硬陶雙耳罐

春秋（公元前 770～前 476 年）

高 12.2、口徑 9.7、底徑 11.1 厘米

直口，斜肩，折腹，平底。器身上斂下收，中間外突。肩部置豎狀環形雙繫。肩部至上腹部飾三道箭羽紋，其間有若干細弦紋。下腹部拍印方格紋。

三五　印紋硬陶雙耳罐

春秋（公元前 770～前 476 年）

高 16.1、口徑 10.7、底徑 14.8 厘米

此罐形如魚簍，腹部下垂，以豎狀環形雙繫對稱，上下協調，造型別致。口沿處有若干旋坯痕，肩腹部飾雲雷紋。

三六　印紋硬陶三繫罐

春秋（公元前 770～前 476 年）

高 5.9、口徑 10、底徑 8.3 厘米

直口，斜肩，鼓腹，平底。肩部置三個爬形獸，用作罐繫。灰色胎。肩腹部飾三道斜方格紋，以弦紋相隔。此罐係輪製成型，再拍印紋飾，製作精良。

三七　印紋硬陶罐

春秋（公元前 770～前 476 年）

高 29.3、口徑 18.3、底徑 19.8 厘米

低領，口沿外翻，豐肩，鼓腹，平底。灰褐色胎體。肩部貼飾兩個 "S" 紋，以幾何形曲折紋作爲主題紋飾，上下飾水波紋。下腹部爲斜方格填綫紋。

三八　印紋硬陶罐

春秋（公元前 770～前 476 年）

高 40.7、口徑 20.5、底徑 22 厘米

敞口，短頸，聳肩，弧腹，平底。灰胎。肩腹部飾豎狀 "S" 紋，下腹部拍印斜方格紋。

三九　印紋硬陶罐

春秋（公元前 770～前 476 年）

高 59.8、口徑 25.2、底徑 24.3 厘米

敞口，縮頸，聳肩，弧腹，平底。胎體灰褐色。以菱形紋爲主題，上下拍印斜方格紋。此器高大，造型渾厚，爲同時代印紋硬陶中所少見。

四〇　印紋硬陶雙繫罐

春秋（公元前 770～前 476 年）

高 19.8、口徑 14.2、底徑 14.3 厘米

矮口，豐肩，弧腹，平底。兩側置泥條絞形豎狀耳。肩部有一道凸弦紋，腹部以水波紋作主題紋飾，下腹爲豎狀箭羽紋。胎體灰褐，器型圓渾。

四一　印紋硬陶人物紋罐
春秋（公元前 770～前 476 年）

高 13.3、口徑 13.5、底徑 14.3 厘米

翻唇，斜頸，聳肩，弧腹，平底。深灰色胎。通體拍印細方格紋，然後在方格紋上飾六個舞蹈狀的人物紋。這在同類器物中極爲少見，非常難得。

四二　印紋硬陶雙繫壺
春秋（公元前 770～前 476 年）

高 16.1、口徑 12.2、底徑 12 厘米

敞口，長頸，豐肩，鼓腹，平底。器身兩側爲豎條狀雙繫。前後貼飾出脊雙環，環與壺身相連，無實際作用，僅作裝飾。深灰色胎體。頸部飾有數道弦紋，器身拍印雲雷交叉紋。

四三　印紋硬陶罐
春秋（公元前 770～前 476 年）

高 15.8、口徑 16、底 17.7 厘米

平口，寬沿，溜肩，鼓腹，平底。胎體灰黑。通體飾米篩紋。

四四　印紋硬陶罐
春秋（公元前 770～前 476 年）

高 19、口徑 18.8、底徑 19.2 厘米

平口，寬沿，溜肩，鼓腹，平底。肩部貼飾三個三角形。胎體深褐。肩腹部以水波紋作主題裝飾，下腹部飾箭羽紋。

四五　印紋硬陶雙繫罐
春秋（公元前 770～前 476 年）

高 13.2、口徑 12.9、底徑 12.6 厘米

短口，斜肩，折腹，平底。環形雙繫，前後貼飾“S”紋。灰褐色胎。肩部飾一週水波紋與箭羽紋，下腹部飾若干道水波紋。

四六　印紋硬陶鳥耳罐
春秋（公元前 770～前 476 年）

高 13.2、口徑 9.4、底徑 15.4 厘米

斂口，豐肩，鼓腹，平底。黃褐色胎。口沿處有若干弦紋，肩腹部拍印方格交叉紋，下腹部飾回紋。左右的雙繫爲倒立的鳥，鳥尾呈環形作繫，將實用性與藝術性完美結合，非常巧妙。

四七　印紋硬陶罐
春秋（公元前 770～前 476 年）

高 19.1、口徑 18.5、底徑 17.4 厘米

捲唇，短頸，溜肩，鼓腹，平底。胎體灰黑。肩腹部置四條出脊。肩腹部飾箭羽紋，下腹拍印兩道方格紋與網格紋。

四八　印紋硬陶雙繫罐
春秋（公元前 770～前 476 年）

高 19、口徑 17、底徑 18.5 厘米

平口，寬沿，溜肩，鼓腹，平底。雙繫呈環狀高翹。深灰色胎體。通體拍飾編織紋。

四九　印紋硬陶瓿
春秋（公元前 770～前 476 年）

高 14.5、口徑 9.5、底徑 13.6 厘米

斂口，斜肩，鼓腹，平底。褐色胎。肩部左右爲豎條狀出脊，前後貼飾“S”紋。口沿處有若干道弦紋，肩部飾水波紋，下腹部拍印網格紋。

五〇　印紋硬陶四繫罐

春秋（公元前 770～前 476 年）

高 11.6、口徑 8.8、底徑 11.8 厘米

直口，豐肩，鼓腹，平底。肩部置四隻獸形繫，形象生動。胎體呈深褐色。上腹部飾三道箭羽紋，下腹部拍印回紋。

五一　印紋硬陶雙耳罐

春秋（公元前 770～前 476 年）

高 13.2、口徑 10、底徑 9.5 厘米

斂口，斜肩，鼓腹，平底。兩側置獸頭狀環形雙耳。褐色胎。通體拍印蔴布紋。器型獨特，較爲少見。

五二　印紋硬陶雙繫量

春秋（公元前 770～前 476 年）

高 15.8、口徑 17.5×17、底徑 17 厘米

方口，圓腹，平底。左右置雙龍，前後爲粘貼豎形雙繫。深褐色胎。通體拍印箭羽紋。

五三　印紋硬陶四繫罐

春秋（公元前 770～前 476 年）

高 10.9、口徑 8.3、底徑 11.5 厘米

直口，溜肩，鼓腹，平底。肩腹部置四個獸形繫。褐色胎體。肩腹部飾四條帶狀水波紋與弦紋，腹部拍印菱形塡綫紋。

五四　印紋硬陶四繫罐

春秋（公元前 770～前 476 年）

高 11.5、口徑 10.5、底徑 12.3 厘米

撇口，斜肩，鼓腹，平底。肩部置四環形繫,繫兩側均貼飾"S"紋。灰胎。通體飾五道水波紋，用弦紋相隔。

五五　印紋硬陶罐

春秋（公元前 770～前 476 年）

高 15.6、口徑 15.6、底徑 17 厘米

撇口，豐肩，弧腹，平底。胎體發黑。紋飾分上下兩部分，上腹部爲菱形塡綫紋，下腹部拍印回紋。頸肩部飾若干弦紋。

五六　印紋硬陶罐

春秋（公元前 770～前 476 年）

高 35.9、口徑 18、底徑 18.5 厘米

撇口，短頸，聳肩，弧腹，平底。胎體黃褐色。頸部飾弦紋，通體飾回紋,罐身中部飾一週菱形"田"字紋。

五七　印紋硬陶罍

春秋（公元前 770～前 476 年）

高 46、口徑 24.8、底徑 26 厘米

撇口，短頸，溜肩，弧腹，平底。褐色胎體。頸部有若干弦紋，罍身上部拍印曲折紋，下部爲編織紋。器身高大，製作精良。

五八　印紋硬陶罍

春秋（公元前 770～前 476 年）

高 42.4、口徑 16.8、底徑 19.8 厘米

撇口，縮頸，溜肩，弧腹，平底。胎體灰黃。頸肩部飾若干弦紋，上腹部拍印編織紋，下腹部飾網格紋。

五九　印紋硬陶罍

春秋（公元前 770～前 476 年）

高 33.3、口徑 15.1、底徑 19 厘米

撇口，短頸，聳肩，弧腹，平底。頸部飾弦紋，罍身通體飾回紋，中部飾一週菱形紋。

六〇　印紋硬陶雙耳筒形罐

春秋（公元前 770～前 476 年）

高 15.5、口徑 10.2、底徑 3.7 厘米

矮口，平肩，斜腹，平底。環形豎狀雙耳。褐色胎體。肩部貼飾"S"紋，飾

有若干弦紋。罐身上端飾水波紋，下部拍印雲雷紋。

六一　印紋硬陶罐

春秋（公元前770～前476年）

高26.5、口徑14.5、底徑13厘米

敞口，縮頸，圓肩，弧腹，平底。黃褐色胎。通體拍印蔴布紋。器型較爲少見。

六二　印紋硬陶罐

春秋（公元前770～前476年）

高43.9、口徑18、底徑17.2厘米

捲脣，短頸，溜肩，弧腹，平底。深褐色胎體。兩側貼飾豎狀出脊，頸部飾弦紋，肩部爲水波紋，腹部以下拍印菱形填綫紋。器身高大，形如鵝卵。

六三　印紋硬陶雙繫罐

春秋（公元前770～前476年）

高50.9、口徑15、底徑20厘米

口沿寬平，折肩，弧腹，平底。灰褐色胎。罐身上部飾水波紋，下部拍印箭羽紋。器型非常少見。

六四　印紋硬陶罐

春秋（公元前770～前476年）

高22.2、口徑14.6、底徑14.9厘米

大口，口沿外撇，斜肩，弧腹，平底。胎體灰黃。上腹部拍印米篩紋，下腹部拍飾蔴布紋。

六五　印紋硬陶罐

春秋（公元前770～前476年）

高49.8、口徑21.1、底徑22.3厘米

平口，豐肩，斜腹，平底。深褐色胎體。上腹部拍飾方格交叉紋，下腹部拍印蔴布紋。

六六　印紋硬陶三足鼎

戰國（公元前475～前221年）

高8.7、口徑9.9厘米

平口，斜肩，垂腹，平底，三足外撇。深灰色胎。通體飾小方格紋。

六七　印紋硬陶貫耳罐（十件）

戰國（公元前475～前221年）

高4.6~3、口徑4.1~2.3、底徑5~2.7厘米

斂口，斜肩，垂腹，平底。胎體多爲褐色，也有灰色。左右置兩個筒形穿帶的貫耳。通體拍印蔴布紋。

六八　印紋硬陶倉

戰國（公元前475～前221年）

高19.6、口徑18.1、底徑17.8厘米

拱形蓋，平口，弧腹，平底。倉的一端爲四檔梯子，梯子中間開一方形窗口。胎體黃中帶褐。通體拍印網格紋。此器爲研究當時糧倉的重要物證。

六九　印紋硬陶倉

戰國（公元前475～前221年）

高18.2、口徑13.6、底徑14厘米

捲脣，斜肩，弧腹，平底。倉的一端爲四檔梯子，梯子中間開一方形窗口。兩側貼飾環狀雲紋耳。灰黑色胎。通體拍印編織紋。

七〇　灰陶插座

戰國（公元前475～前221年）

高12.2、口徑10.6、底徑35.8厘米

短平口，斜肩，直腹，內底空。灰陶胎外部泛黑。通體飾方格加"S"紋。

七一　灰陶雙繫罐

戰國（公元前475～前221年）

高 11、口徑 8.7、底徑 13 厘米

直口，短頸，豐肩，斜腹，平底。兩側置半圓形繫，繫的外圍爲六邊形。灰陶胎外部泛黑。腹下部有弦紋三週，下部飾"S"紋。

七二　印紋硬陶帶把罐（三件）

戰國（公元前 475～前 221 年）

高 12.5、口徑 8.9、底徑 11.6 厘米

高 6.6、口徑 5.4、底徑 5.4 厘米

高 5.2、口徑 4.2、底徑 4.8 厘米

此三件帶把罐的造型基本一致，均爲斂口，溜肩，弧腹，平底。罐的一端均置"S"形把。黃褐色胎。通體拍印麻布紋。所不同的是，最大一件的另一端有一活動的環。

七三　印紋硬陶筒形罐（三件）

戰國（公元前 475～前 221 年）

高 13.2、口徑 8.7、底徑 12.8 厘米

高 10.3、口徑 6.9、底徑 6.3 厘米

高 9.9、口徑 7.1、底徑 7 厘米

此三件筒形罐的造型基本一致，斂口，豐肩，弧腹，平底。罐肩部兩側均置一圓筒形穿帶貫耳。不同的是，大的一件腹部下垂，小的兩件下腹內收。黃褐色胎體。通體飾麻布紋。

七四　硬陶虎子

戰國（公元前 475～前 221 年）

高 19.9、口徑 9、底徑 18.6 厘米

半圓形提梁，一端爲瓦片狀流，平口，溜肩，弧腹，平底。褐色胎體。素面無紋。造型別致，極爲少見。

七五　印紋硬陶雙繫罐

戰國（公元前 475～前 221 年）

高 9.3、口徑 13.5、底徑 10.3 厘米

大口，弧腹，平底。兩側爲帶環雙繫，繫上貼飾"S"紋。黃褐色胎體。通體拍印麻布紋。

七六　灰陶虎子

漢（公元前 206～公元 220 年）

高 17.4、長 27.2、口徑 5.8 厘米

口略敞，折沿，圓唇，短直頸，器身呈圓桶形。背部有兩個橋形寬繫，腹有四隻長方形足，既可方便懸掛，也可平穩放置，又能在握手時不會滑脫。器物實用，簡潔大方。

七七　灰陶井

漢（公元前 206～公元 220 年）

高 10.2、口徑 11 厘米

口微斂，口沿相對寬平，斜腹，器身略下鼓，平底。器物外壁用繩索紋作網狀裝飾。

七八　釉陶羊首虎子

東漢（公元 25～220 年）

高 18、長 23.7、口徑 4.3 厘米

斂口，短直頸，器身呈圓桶形。器口上部飾一公山羊頭，圓目外突，豎耳，兩圈曲羊角健碩有力，緊貼器身。背部爲一粗繩索紋提梁。器身上用棱紋夾多條錐刺點組成的短弧綫表示羊毛。四肢用半弧形曲綫勾勒來表現其健碩。器物表現手法多樣，生動傳神。器身外施青褐色釉，腹底不施釉，釉層積厚處呈黑褐色。

七九　釉陶虎子

東漢（公元 25～220 年）

高 15.7、長 24.8、口徑 6 厘米

敞口，圓唇，略縮頸，器身呈圓桶形。器口上部飾一虎頭，虎目圓睜，虎耳直豎。器背爲一粗繩索紋提梁，提梁後爲一捲曲虎尾，腹下四虎足踞臥。施褐黃色釉，釉層較厚，光潔圓潤。

八〇　釉陶虎子

東漢（公元 25～220 年）

高 20.2、長 26.1、口徑 5.3 厘米

敞口，短直頸，器身前粗後細，略呈圓桶形，腹下四虎足踞臥。器身上部飾一露齒笑面虎，虎背用多個近"W"形紋前後排列作爲裝飾。器背爲一粗繩索紋提梁，器身用多條曲綫裝飾。器物施青黃色釉，釉層較厚，圓潤光亮。

瓷　器　篇

八一　原始瓷雙繫尊

商（公元前 1600～前 1046 年）

高 19.8、口徑 24、底徑 15 厘米

敞口，縮頸，斜肩下折，腹斜收，小平底，圈足外撇。肩部飾兩組對稱的複繫。與器壁連接處上下各有一個突起的圓點。器物上部用三組弦紋，中間夾有二組四條曲綫組成的水波紋作裝飾。施淡黃色青釉，底部燒成火候底。

八二　原始瓷豆

西周（公元前 1046～前 771 年）

高 6.1、口徑 13.8、底徑 7.5 厘米

蕭山長河塘子堰(現屬杭州市濱江區)出土

敞口，厚圓唇捲沿，縮頸，肩斜下折腹，淺弧腹，小平底，厚圈足略外撇，外底略呈玉璧形。肩部飾一組弦紋夾多條斜短綫狀錐刺紋。內外壁都施青褐色釉，釉層較厚且光亮，釉層有冰裂現象，積釉厚處呈黑褐色，外底無釉。

八三　原始瓷蓋盂

西周（公元前 1046～前 771 年）

通高 4.5、口徑 5.7、底徑 4.2 厘米

侈口，略縮頸，扁折腹，斜腹內收，凹弧底，矮圈足。圓拱形蓋，蓋上飾並列粘連的橋形複紐，繫與蓋粘連處上有"S"形貼飾。口沿外側上凹曲處有三處貼有"S"紋，呈三角形對稱，其中兩處爲單個橫向"S"紋，另一處爲並排兩個豎向"S"紋。"S"紋中間夾斜短綫狀錐刺紋飾。施黃褐色釉，釉層有冰裂現象。

八四　原始瓷鼎

春秋早期（公元前 770～前 677 年）

高 16.1、口徑 21.4、足高 4.1 厘米

蕭山長山出土

敞口，縮頸，溜肩，鼓腹，小平底，三柱足。腰腹部飾有七圈錐刺紋，前後有兩個蛇形貼飾，左右的雙耳已殘。器身內外施青黃釉，釉色均勻光亮。胎質堅硬，火候較高。

八五　原始瓷盂

春秋早期（公元前 770～前 677 年）

高 7.2、口徑 11.5、底徑 9.5 厘米

蕭山長山出土

直口，折肩，腹弧收，內底略弧凹，外底平。內底旋圈明顯，肩部貼對稱的兩組"S"紋，每組"S"紋爲兩個，中間用繩紋相連成雙繫。器上部有兩圈呈塊狀分佈的錐刺紋。施青褐色釉，釉層厚處呈黑褐色，有細小開片現象。

八六　原始瓷尊

春秋（公元前 770～前 476 年）

高 23.4、口徑 21.5、底徑 18.5 厘米

大敞口，長直頸，鼓腹，小平底，高圈足外撇，圈足口沿下折，呈倒盤口狀。腹部突起處飾"S"紋。造型規整，內外通體施青黃色厚釉，縮釉明顯。

八七　原始瓷雙繫罐

春秋（公元前770～前476年）

高 19.2、口徑 15.6、底徑 17.9 厘米

敞口，捲唇，縮頸，鼓肩，腹向下斜收，平底。器身飾一對橋形繫，每繫有三個小繫並排粘連組成，以梯狀形綫條紋飾作主紋飾。施青黃色釉，釉層有磨損，但胎釉結合較好。

八八　原始瓷鑒

春秋（公元前770～前476年）

高 10、口徑 33、底徑 16.5 厘米

口沿寬平，斜腹，小平底，三獸足。口沿和器身上飾有成行排列的"S"紋，寬口沿上有四處呈對稱的多條短綫組成的錐刺紋，其下的腹壁上部皆貼有模印鋪獸啣環。內外施釉，色深黃，釉層飽滿，縮釉明顯。其造型工整大方，做工講究，仿同期的青銅器而製，給人以凝重莊嚴之感。

八九　原始瓷簋

春秋（公元前770～前476年）

高 6.9、口徑 21.5、底徑 18.4 厘米

口略敞，淺直腹，平底，環形圈足。方形耳貼飾，耳上飾斜方格紋。器外壁以斜方格紋內加圓珠紋爲主紋飾。脫釉，火候較低。

九〇　原始瓷壺

春秋（公元前770～前476年）

高 19.2、口徑 9、底徑 11 厘米

斂口，溜肩，腹略鼓，平底，器身呈扁橢圓形。左右爲一對蛇形貼飾繫。頸部以旋紋爲主，腰身和上腹部密布水波紋。施青褐色釉，脫釉較多。

九一　原始瓷罐

春秋（公元前770～前476年）

高 26.4、口徑 23、底徑 20.5 厘米

侈口，弧形厚唇，圓溜肩，鼓腹，弧收腹，平底。口沿下飾四圈水波紋，器身上佈滿葉脈狀紋飾，中夾三圈圓珠紋。施青釉，胎釉結合較好，有光亮感。

九二　原始瓷盤

戰國（公元前475～前221年）

高 12.2、口徑 36.5、底徑 35.2 厘米

口沿寬平，淺直腹，平底，三蹄足外撇。三管狀耳，上有弦紋作裝飾。口沿上飾滿變形"S"紋，腹壁上用兩圈突起的繩索紋將變形回紋圖案分爲上下兩部分。足上各有一個圓孔。胎質呈火紅色。釉脫落，足部火候較低。

九三　原始瓷薰

戰國（公元前475～前221年）

高 47.2、口徑 9.6、底徑 17.2 厘米

口略敞，方唇，長直頸，鼓腹，平底。口沿下有一圈加厚，頸部飾兩條對稱葉脈紋。頸以下飾有五圈繩索紋，猶如五道箍。肩腹部有三圈銳角三角形出煙孔。施黃色青釉，釉層較薄，縮釉明顯。

九四　原始瓷薰

戰國（公元前475～前221年）

高 40.2、口徑 9.9、底徑 17.5 厘米

口微斂，方唇，弧形長頸，球狀鼓腹，平底。口沿下飾有一圈弦紋，頸部以下飾有五組弦紋，腹部有三組三角形組成的出煙孔。施黃色青釉。

九五　原始瓷烤爐

戰國（公元前475～前221年）

高 10.4、口徑 34.3 厘米

口沿寬平，腹漸斜收，外器底略弧形，三足稍外撇。器內壁有短柱支撐寬平口沿，內底有突出大泡。外壁有四個對稱鋪

首貼飾繫，口沿和腹壁上佈滿"S"紋。器外底及足不施釉，外壁施釉較勻，釉色圓潤有光。此器較大而少見。

九六　原始瓷雙繫大罐

戰國（公元前475～前221年）

高26.2、口徑20.3、底徑22.6厘米

直口，短頸，溜肩，鼓腹，下部弧收，平底。左右半環形耳立於佈滿回紋的方塊紋飾上。器身上部和下部各有兩圈直短綫狀突稜，間距極爲均勻。兩稜之間爲半圓弧形，有如條條溝壑。器物施釉均勻，色較黃且圓潤，縮釉明顯。器物保存完好，造型極爲規整，且在燒製過程中沒有變形，歷經千年無損，實屬難得。

九七　原始瓷雙繫罐

戰國（公元前475～前221年）

高18.9、口徑14、底徑13.4厘米

蕭山長河塘子堰（現屬杭州市濱江區）出土

大直口，圓肩，弧收腹，平底。飾對稱橋形繫，繫內有環。繫兩側各有一塊橫短綫條狀組成錐刺紋。肩部和腹部各飾有短綫狀直稜紋一圈。施黃色青釉，釉色潤潔富有光澤，釉厚處略呈黃褐色。

九八　原始瓷瓿

戰國（公元前475～前221年）

通高28、口徑15.8、蓋徑19、底徑20.6厘米

短直口，圓肩，鼓腹，下腹弧收，平底。器蓋略扁平，佈滿"S"紋，中間爲一橋形紐。器身飾對稱半環形繫，繫上各有四個突角，啣環可動。以四圈突寬稜分隔器身的"S"紋。施青黃色釉，縮釉明顯，釉層光亮。器物較大，極爲規整，保存完好，是難得的精品。

九九　原始瓷洗

戰國（公元前475～前221年）

高10.6、口徑22.1、底徑16厘米

平口，直頸，折腹，腹弧收，外底略平，置三矮蹄足。兩蒲扇形附耳上佈滿變形"S"紋，器身上以三圈繩索紋夾三圈"S"紋作主題紋飾。內外施青褐色釉，釉色圓潤有光澤，胎釉結合良好。

一〇〇　原始瓷雙繫罐

戰國（公元前475～前221年）

高20.6、口徑17、底徑16.8厘米

直口，圓鼓肩，弧收腹，平底。兩側貼鋪首繫一對。造型規整，內壁旋紋明顯。內外施釉，肩部施釉明顯厚於其他部分。

一〇一　原始瓷釉下彩鈴

戰國（公元前475～前221年）

高8.8、底徑10.4厘米

器物造型規整，呈半球形，底部爲中空圓餅形，器身中空。頂部爲半環形紐，紐旁飾有"S"紋。器身有四圈弦紋，爲釉下褐彩。這對研究我國釉下彩的歷史提供了很好的實證。

一〇二　原始瓷錞于

戰國（公元前475～前221年）

高39.4、口徑16.3、底徑18.4厘米

敞口，略束腰，鼓腹，假矮圈足，平底，底上有紐。近口沿處有兩圈凹弦紋夾一圈連珠紋，外壁上有一直突稜自器口及底。底圈沿上呈繩索形紋飾。施黃色青釉。

一〇三　原始瓷句鑃

戰國（公元前475～前221年）

高48.5、直徑22.9、柄長14.4厘米

口沿呈凹弧形，器身橫截面呈橢圓形，向柄部漸斜收。柄部橫截面呈長方形，

分兩段，也漸向頂部收尖。器柄近底處施回紋，器身上以兩圈弦紋夾飾四圈回紋，再添一圈三角形紋，三角形紋內滿飾"S"形紋。施黃色青釉。

一〇四　原始瓷龍

戰國（公元前475～前221年）

高7.5、長18.2、厚1.9厘米

龍身整體呈"S"形，口微張，昂首後仰，形體彎曲，龍尾捲曲上翹，似騰雲狀。器身兩面都滿飾"S"紋。施青黃色釉。背部有一穿孔。

一〇五　原始瓷壺

戰國（公元前475～前221年）

通高33.8、口徑12.4、蓋徑16.1、底徑17.2厘米

器身子口，束頸，溜肩，下腹弧收，平底。拱形蓋，蓋近中心處有三圈回紋，近邊緣處貼飾三個豎立的小紐，紐中有小孔，紐外有兩圈回紋。三獸耳貼飾以一圈弦紋爲界，其下佈滿回紋。腹部有旋紋。蓋頂和外壁施黃色青釉，器內近口沿處也有一層流釉。

一〇六　原始瓷壺

戰國（公元前475～前221年）

通高36.8、口徑13.5、蓋徑17、底徑19厘米

器身子口，束頸，溜肩，下腹弧收，平底。拱形蓋，蓋近中心處有三圈回紋，近邊緣處貼飾三個豎立的小紐，紐中有小孔，紐外有兩圈回紋。三獸耳貼飾以一圈弦紋爲界，其下佈滿回紋。腹部有旋紋。蓋頂和外壁施深黃色青釉，器內近口沿處有一層流釉。

一〇七　原始瓷雙耳瓿

戰國（公元前475～前221年）

高33、口徑22.5、底徑25.8厘米

敞口，寬弧沿，短直頸，圓肩，鼓腹，平底。肩腹部上飾對稱獸耳，啣環可動。器身滿飾"S"紋。胎呈赭紅色，素面無釉。此器較大且造型規整。

一〇八　原始瓷匜

戰國（公元前475～前221年）

高17.8、口徑36、底徑21厘米

口微斂，流部似半個管狀弧形外展，下腹部斜收，平底。一側有羊角形耳飾，以短綫直稜紋作器身裝飾。施黃色青釉。

一〇九　原始瓷提梁盉

戰國（公元前475～前221年）

高17.3、口徑6.5厘米

短直口，廣圓肩，下腹略弧收，平底，三蹄足外撇。龍形提梁，梁上有扉稜，獸頭上有小孔。蓋上有橋形紐。器身飾滿"S"紋，以弦紋作分隔。施青黃色釉。此器造型古拙，集藝術性與實用性爲一體。

一一〇　原始瓷雙繫罐

戰國（公元前475～前221年）

高14.1、口徑9、底徑9.8厘米

短直口，廣圓肩，深直腹，近底處內收，平底。肩部飾兩獸耳繫，腹部有一圈豎條紋。施青黃色釉。

一一一　原始瓷蓋碗（六件）

戰國（公元前475～前221年）

最大件通高11.2、口徑12.2、蓋徑13.7、底徑7.7厘米

子口，腹弧收，平底。拱形蓋，中間爲一橋形紐，紐旁有一圓洞，以多圈寬弦稜紋裝飾蓋面。施黃色青釉，蓋頂的釉層厚而有光澤。

一一二 原始瓷勺（兩件）

戰國（公元前 475～前 221 年）

柄長 5.1、孔徑 1.6、寬 7.7 厘米

此勺近畚箕形，底略平，器沿上翹。器柄中空，可裝小木柄。通體施釉。

一一三 原始瓷匜

戰國（公元前 475～前 221 年）

高 7.2、口徑 13.7、底徑 6.5 厘米

蕭山長河塘子堰（現屬杭州市濱江區）出土

斂口，略鼓腹，下腹弧收，內底略弧形，外底平。外器底和內壁有明顯的旋紋。器口沿一側捏成小流，對稱一側有彎曲羊角形貼飾。施青釉。

一一四 原始瓷直口小罐（兩件）

戰國（公元前 475～前 221 年）

大件高 9.8、口徑 7.3、底徑 10.2 厘米

直口，弧形唇，直頸，廣平肩，折腹漸收，小平底，三矮足。肩和上腹均飾水波紋。施黃色青釉。

一一五 原始瓷鼎

戰國（公元前 475～前 221 年）

通高 18.3、口徑 14、蓋徑 16.7 厘米

子口，長方形附耳，耳較外敞，深直腹，圜底，柱狀三足外撇。拱形蓋，頂有橋形紐，蓋緣貼塑三個豎立小紐，以三組弦紋分隔"S"紋。

一一六 原始瓷獸面鼎

戰國（公元前 475～前 221 年）

高 15.3、口徑 14.2、足高 3.6 厘米

斂口，深直腹，近底處斜收，小平底，下爲三獸足。器身飾一對長方形附耳，其中獸面的眼睛和角特別突出；相對一側是一蛇形貼飾，緊緊趴在器身上，兩眼突出。外器壁飾"S"紋，中部有一圈突棱把器

物規整地一分爲二。器物釉色深黃。此器保存完好，對研究當時的風俗和藝術發展水平提供了很好的實物證據。

一一七 原始瓷鼎

戰國（公元前 475～前 221 年）

通高 13.6、口徑 15 厘米

蕭山長河塘子堰（現屬杭州市濱江區）出土

喇叭形口，肩內收，束腰，略鼓腹，圜底，三高蹄足外撇。兩耳貼在口沿內側。器內壁有旋紋。施青黃色釉。

一一八 原始瓷鼎

戰國（公元前 475～前 221 年）

通高 19.2、口徑 20.7 厘米

直口，肩寬平內折，束腰，腹下垂外鼓，小平底，三柱狀足外撇。器內壁肩上置兩半環形立耳緊貼口沿。內外施青黃色釉，器內壁比外壁施釉厚而均勻。

一一九 原始瓷鼎

戰國（公元前 475～前 221 年）

通高 20.4、口徑 17.3、蓋徑 19.5 厘米

子口，深垂腹，平底，三足外撇。器蓋表面佈滿"S"紋，由三條突起寬棱將畫面分爲四個部分。蓋正中爲一橋形紐，近邊緣處爲三立紐，紐上各穿有兩個小孔。兩側爲長方形附耳。通體施青黃色釉。

一二○ 原始瓷鼎

戰國（公元前 475～前 221 年）

通高 20.5、口徑 18、蓋徑 19.8 厘米

子口，深直腹，圜底，三足外撇。器蓋表面佈滿"S"紋，由三條突起蠅索紋將畫面分爲四個部分。中間以多個同心圓作裝飾，近耳處爲三個帶孔的立紐。器外壁皆施釉，器身流釉明顯，內壁無釉。

一二一　原始瓷鼎

戰國（公元前 475～前 221 年）

通高 10.8、口徑 9、蓋徑 10.5 厘米

子口，短直腹，圓弧底，三蹄足外撇。拱形器蓋上以三道寬稜作裝飾，中間是數個同心圓，外沿上立三個門洞形稍向外斜的立紐。兩長方形附耳略外撇。器身中間有一圈突起的寬稜作裝飾。除了外底，其餘部位皆施青黃色釉。

一二二　原始瓷鼎

戰國（公元前 475～前 221 年）

通高 11.4、口徑 10.5、蓋徑 11.9 厘米

子口，略鼓腹，半球形底，外底爲小平底，三蹄足略外撇。蓋略呈拱形，以寬突弦紋夾"S"紋裝飾爲主，邊緣立三個半環形有洞立紐。兩側爲長方形附耳，口沿下有一圈"S"紋和一圈弦紋。除了外底，其餘部位皆施青釉，釉層較厚，而且圓潤有光澤。

一二三　原始瓷甗

戰國（公元前 475～前 221 年）

高 12.4、口徑 15.1、底徑 6.8 厘米

斂口，平唇，腹向下斜收，平底，底有圓洞。口部比器身稍厚，口沿下有長方形橫檔，便於提拿。通體施青釉。

一二四　原始瓷虎子

戰國（公元前 475～前 221 年）

高 17.8、口徑 6、底徑 13.1 厘米

上身半球形，下腹斜收，平底。橋形提梁。柱狀口略外敞，上爲一缺口。施青黃色釉，釉層較厚，縮釉明顯。

一二五　原始瓷虎子

戰國（公元前 475～前 221 年）

高 17.8、口徑 6.5、底徑 13.5 厘米

器身頂部有一圓形小口，口沿稍寬平，廣溜肩，圓鼓腹，下腹弧收，平底。流呈圓筒形，上有缺口，口部略敞。器身置半環形提梁。施青黃色釉，釉色較均勻。

一二六　原始瓷虎子

戰國（公元前 475～前 221 年）

高 18.9、口徑 7.5、底徑 13 厘米

器身上部半球形，鼓腹，下腹弧收，平底。弓形提梁。器身兩側開口。一側爲獸形頭部，有兩錐角，開小方口；另一側爲喇叭形大口。施青黃色釉。

一二七　原始瓷豆（兩件）

戰國（公元前 475～前 221 年）

高 11.8、口徑 17.8、底徑 11 厘米

敞口，圓唇，淺弧腹，底略平，高柄，喇叭形圈足底座。器內壁旋紋明顯，器型規整。施黃色青釉。

一二八　原始瓷帶流罐

戰國（公元前 475～前 221 年）

高 17.8、口徑 15.2、底徑 12.6 厘米

方唇，侈口，短直頸，鼓肩，斜收下腹，平底。一側爲獸形貼飾，一側爲流（出水口）。

一二九　原始瓷雙繫筒形罐（兩件）

戰國（公元前 475～前 221 年）

通高 21.2、口徑 16.8、蓋徑 15、底徑 13.7 厘米

斂口，直腹，近底處斜收，平底。拱形蓋正中爲橋形繫，下壓兩個"S"形貼飾，並飾以多圈同心圓的弦紋。器身上有對稱的獸形貼飾。

一三〇　原始瓷熏爐

戰國至西漢（公元前 475～公元 8 年）

通高 17、口徑 9.4、蓋徑 12.1、底徑

7.2厘米

子口，爐體呈深腹豆形狀，近直腹，內底寬平，倒置淺杯式高圈足。上置拱形蓋，蓋面有兩週三角形鏤孔用作煙孔。紐較高，作兩層圓形寶塔狀，中空，各層均有圓形鏤孔。塔面貼飾三隻小鳥，塔尖昂立一隻大鳥。熏爐外壁飾有水波紋，蓋面以弦紋和足印紋爲主。蓋上飾青釉。

一三一　原始瓷瓿

西漢（公元前206～公元8年）

通高24、口徑9.8、蓋徑11.6、底徑18.5厘米

蕭山北幹山烈士陵園工地出土

笠式蓋，子母口，平唇，溜肩，鼓腹。肩腹部置變形人面紋雙耳，底部有三扁形矮足。灰胎，施半截青黃色釉，下腹露胎處氧化呈赭色。肩腹部飾三道弦紋和兩道水波紋。

一三二　原始瓷熏爐

西漢（公元前206～公元8年）

高15.2、孔徑5.7厘米

拱形蓋與器身粘連在一起，粘連處器沿寬平，腹斜收，平底，三矮蹄足。器頂正中爲一稍大出煙孔，下爲三個對稱稍小的出煙孔，以弦紋夾水波紋滿飾蓋面。青灰色胎，蓋面施黃色青釉，下腹無釉。

一三三　原始瓷熏爐

漢（公元前206～公元220年）

孔徑7.6、高20.1、底徑12.5厘米

器身呈鼓卵形，上半部中部出煙口爲圓斂口，器身向中部連接處鼓起，連接處寬沿外折，下腹斜收，矮圈足外撇，底中空。器上部裝飾共分三層，第一層出煙口下爲一圈連珠紋，下爲鳳鳥紋，第二層爲鳳鳥紋加四個三角形出煙孔，第三層爲對稱的兩個圓形出煙孔。施黃色青釉。

一三四　原始瓷匜

漢（公元前206～公元220年）

高6、口徑11.3 × 12、底徑8.5厘米

蕭山許賢採集

斂口，略鼓腹，外底平，器內外壁有旋痕。器爲長方形，底近圓形。施青褐色釉。

一三五　原始瓷五管瓶

漢（公元前206～公元220年）

高22.8、口徑8.7、底徑10.5厘米

器身可分爲上下兩層。上部敞口，斜唇，縮頸，鼓腹。下部呈穀倉形，對稱貼着四個直筒狀小管，平底。四小管與器身不相通。施青黃色釉。

一三六　原始瓷鼎

漢（公元前206～公元220年）

通高18.5、口徑14.4、蓋徑16.3厘米

蕭山城南出土

子母口，長方形附耳外撇，深腹，圜底，三矮蹄足略外撇。器蓋弧度較大，上飾三扁形穿孔紐。器身有一道突棱。施青黃色釉，器蓋施釉較厚，但胎釉結合不是很好。

一三七　原始瓷長頸瓶

漢（公元前206～公元220年）

高25、口徑5、底徑12.3厘米

直口，長直頸，扁鼓腹，矮圈足，平底。頸部飾弦紋夾多圈細水波紋，腹部以弦紋爲主。施褐色青釉。

一三八　原始瓷井與吊桶

東漢（公元25～220年）

瓷井高17.8、口徑11.1、底徑11.5厘米

吊桶高 5.2、口徑 3.2 厘米

寬口沿下折，斜頸，肩部下折，直腹，平底。器身上有對稱柱洞，飾有多圈寬稜紋。僅口沿和頸肩部施釉。吊桶爲敞口，微縮頸，球狀腹，小平底。

一三九　原始瓷虎子

東漢（公元 25～220 年）

高 16.7、口徑 4.8、底徑 12 厘米

敞口，圓唇，下有一圈圓稜狀突起，短直頸，球狀腹，平底。粗繩索狀提梁下有直柱，繩索兩末端分開三條呈蛇狀貼於器上，飾有細弦紋多組。施半身黃褐色青釉，釉層厚且富有光澤，積釉厚處呈黑褐色，器身有梳狀流釉。

一四〇　褐釉熏爐

東漢（公元 25～220 年）

通高 28、口徑 16.5、蓋徑 19.1、底徑 15 厘米

斂口，圓唇，廣圓肩，略鼓腹，下腹弧收，平底。扁圓蓋正中立一昂首小鳥，鳥外圍依次裝飾有三組弦紋和三組環狀小圓形出煙孔，其中二組出煙孔在正面，一組在側立面。兩側飾半環形耳。器身上佈滿呈環狀分布的小圓形出煙孔以及五組弦紋，其中弦紋以上圓孔分佈較規則有序，下部較亂。器底中部有一圓孔，外圍置一圈圓孔，可用作煙灰的出口。施青褐色釉，蓋頂釉色比器身更深。

一四一　青瓷鍾

東漢（公元 25～220 年）

高 31.1、口徑 15、底徑 14.2 厘米

盤口，直頸，溜肩，鼓腹，下腹斜收，小平底，高圓圈足外撇。肩部飾對稱橋形

耳，耳上有葉脈紋。器身飾兩組弦紋夾一組水波紋。圈足外壁上有折稜，圈足根部有對稱圓孔。胎呈青灰色，施青釉。

一四二　醬釉鍾

東漢（公元 25～220 年）

高 30.3、口徑 14.4、底徑 15.5 厘米

盤口，直頸，溜肩，鼓腹，下腹弧收，小平底，圓圈足外撇。肩部飾對稱橋形耳，耳上有葉脈紋。肩部有兩組弦紋，口沿和足部也有弦紋。圓圈足上有折稜紋。施黃褐色青釉，釉層飽滿，積釉厚處呈黑褐色。

一四三　青瓷五管瓶

東漢（公元 25～220 年）

高 53.4、口徑 5.1、底徑 16.3 厘米

瓶爲三層。上層瓶爲敞口，細弧縮頸，垂鼓腹，中部和下部皆爲罐形，平底。上部和中部皆有四隻小鳥貼於器上，中部有四小瓶立於肩上。五瓶皆通腹。三熊呈托腮狀，坐靠於器身，熊與熊之間有一圓形小孔，並貼飾有一條蠶狀物。胎身有旋紋。施青黃色釉，施釉不及底，有聚釉和流釉現象。

一四四　黑釉五管瓶

東漢（公元 25～220 年）

高 49、底徑 15.5 厘米

蕭山衙前鳳凰村出土

瓶爲三層。上層中部爲盤口壺，四小壺立於二層肩部。五管口皆通腹。瓶中部置有三頭立式熊，形象生動，憨態可掬。下腹略鼓，有旋壞痕，平底。黑胎，施黑釉，晶瑩潤澤。

一四五　黑釉酒具

東漢（公元 25～220 年）

托盤高 3.2、口徑 40.6、底徑 39.5 厘米
鐎斗高 13.2、口徑 17.2、足高 5.2 厘米
耳杯高 3.4、口徑 9.8~5.9、底徑 4.6~
2.8 厘米

托盤爲圓唇，淺斜腹，大平底，底部旋紋明顯。鐎斗爲敞口，圓唇，寬凹形沿，縮頸，溜肩，垂鼓腹，三柱足外撇，柱狀鋬柄。耳杯大小、造型基本一致，圓唇，深弧腹，外底平，雙耳弧形、細長、外折、寬平。整套酒具内外施黑褐色釉，外底皆無釉。

一四六　黑釉盤口壺

東漢（公元 25~220 年）
高 22.6、口徑 11.3、底徑 12 厘米
蕭山北幹山出土

洗口，口沿外撇，縮頸，溜肩，鼓腹，下腹弧收，平底。橋形耳，耳上有十字形紋飾。肩腹部飾有多道弦紋，口沿下有折稜紋。施黑褐色釉，釉色飽滿，施釉不及底。

一四七　越窯青瓷雙繫罐

東漢（公元 25~220 年）
高 10.4、口徑 7.2、底徑 9.1 厘米

直口，圓唇，圓溜肩，鼓腹，平底。肩部飾對稱環形繫。另有兩組弦紋夾一組水波紋。施青釉，基本及底，釉色圓潤有光澤，釉層較均勻，釉面佈滿細小冰裂紋。

一四八　越窯青瓷堆塑罐

三國吳（公元 222~280 年）
高 49.2、口徑 8、底徑 16.2 厘米

器分三層。上部爲小盤口壺形，以四隻飛鳥間隔四座佛像作爲主題紋飾。中部以四小盤口罐貼於主罐上，小罐底與主器不相通，並下垂一柱狀物立於器上。中部與下部連接處呈圓盤狀。中部裝飾亭臺樓閣、胡人、飛鳥、鳳、熊等，各類形象表現得極爲生動多樣，好似瑤臺仙閣。下部爲壇形，以龍紋、佛像裝飾爲主，其下有游魚。施青釉，釉層較均勻，極富光澤，並有流釉現象。

一四九　越窯青瓷虎子

三國吳（公元 222~280 年）
高 16.2、口徑 4.5、長 21 厘米

斂口，斜頸，器身呈啞鈴狀，背部置一虎形貼飾提梁，腹底部有四隻踞臥狀獸足。此器造型生動，施青釉。

一五〇　越窯青瓷洗

三國吳（公元 222~280 年）
高 9.9、口徑 20、底徑 11.8 厘米

侈口，厚唇，口沿寬折，深腹，平底，三獸足。腹部飾鋪首貼飾、斜方格紋和多圈旋紋。通體施青釉。

一五一　褐釉蛙形盂

三國吳（公元 222~280 年）
高 4.6、口徑 2、底徑 4.3 厘米

背部小直口，圓唇，短直頸，扁圓鼓腹，外底略内凹。蛙昂首，閉口，圓睜目，強健四肢呈收縮蓄勢狀，背部以多條弧綫作爲裝飾。施黃褐色青釉，積釉厚處呈黑褐色，釉面圓潤光潔，有細小冰裂紋。

一五二　越窯青瓷虎子

三國吳（公元 222~280 年）
高 17、口徑 5.8、長 23.1 厘米

虎作昂首張口狀。虎頭刻畫細膩生動，毛髮和斑紋用短弧綫和點刺紋表現，鼻、眼、耳寫實生動，背部置繩索狀提梁，尾部捲曲，四肢用突起的塊面和旋紋表現肌肉，腹下有踞臥的四獸足。通體施青釉，釉色圓潤而有光澤。

一五三　越窰青瓷武士俑

西晉（公元265～316年）

高28.9厘米

蕭山城南聯華村出土

頭紮高巾，頂尖，後部翻蓋，巾沿內捲，後有繫紮之飄帶，形狀酷似紹興烏氈帽。身著斜襟寬袖大袍。右手持劍，左手持盾。雙膝跪地。珠狀目，隆鼻，嘴部爲兩小孔，唇上陰刻翹鬚，神情蕭穆。灰青色胎，露胎處氧化呈褐色。身中空，通體施青釉，局部釉層肥厚而光亮。巾沿、衣袖、背部等多處有條狀斜方格鋸齒紋。

一五四　越窰青瓷仕女俑

西晉（公元265～316年）

高26.3厘米

蕭山城南聯華村出土

頭挽髮髻，用陰綫刻出髮際。臥蠶眉，珠目，隆鼻，小嘴，耳部有珠狀耳飾。臉部豐盈，神情安詳。雙膝跪地。身著斜襟長袍。衣袖、背部有若干條狀斜方格紋。右手握一把長方形扇子，左手懷抱一小孩。小孩頭挽雙髻，著寬袖衣，左手抱一瓜楞球形玩具。胎色灰青，身中空，露胎處氧化呈褐色。通體施青釉，頭部釉質尤佳，瑩潤而光亮。

一五五　越窰青瓷男俑

西晉（公元265～316年）

高23.9厘米

頭紮方巾，巾沿內捲，後部爲方摺，前部兩隻巾角上揚。上身著交領寬袖上衣，下身爲寬鬆大褲。濃眉，珠目，高鼻，嘴角上揚，短鬚，面帶微笑。雙手置於袖內，再交於胸前。身中空。通體施青釉。

一五六　越窰青瓷男俑

西晉（公元265～316年）

高23.3厘米

頭紮方巾，巾角束髮後上揚。上身著寬袖長交領上衣，下身穿寬鬆大褲。濃眉，珠目，高鼻，嘴角內收，面帶微笑。雙手置於袖內，再交於胸前。身中空。通體施青釉。

一五七　越窰青瓷女俑

西晉（公元265～316年）

高19.6厘米

頭部髮髻垂於一側，身著長對領寬袖長袍。柳葉眉，杏目，高鼻，小嘴，面帶微笑。雙手置於袖內，再交於胸前。身中空。通體施青釉。

一五八　越窰青瓷女俑

西晉（公元265～316年）

高19.1厘米

頭部髮髻垂於一側，身著對領寬袖長袍。柳葉眉，杏目，高鼻，小嘴，面帶微笑。雙手置於袖內，再交於胸前。身中空。通體施青釉。

一五九　越窰青瓷男女俑（四件）

西晉（公元265～316年）

高23.9～19.1厘米

四件男女俑均面帶微笑，神態安詳，雙手相交於袖內，再置於胸前，好似列隊相迎。器物釉色潤澤，是當時青瓷燒造技術的代表作，對研究當時的服飾也有幫助。

一六〇　越窰青瓷樽

西晉（公元265～316年）

通高18.4、口徑18.3、蓋徑20.6、底徑18.8厘米

子口，深直腹，平底。器蓋呈圓拱形，正中立一扁圓形紐，紐有小孔，蓋面飾多圈弦紋和兩圈寬帶狀斜方格紋。器身有一

圈弦紋，器身內部坯旋紋明顯。通體施青釉，釉色圓潤光亮，微顯褐色，釉面有細小開片。器外底和蓋沿下有支燒痕。

一六一　越窰青瓷獅形插座

西晉（公元265～316年）

高11、長17.3厘米

獅呈俯臥仰首狀，背部有一管狀插孔。毛髮用細綫雕刻而成，尾部呈下垂芭蕉葉狀，頭部刻畫細膩。整體造型生動準確，對研究當時藝術的表現方式提供了很好的實物材料。器身通體施青釉，釉層匀潤，充分展示了當時燒瓷的高超技藝。

一六二　越窰青瓷虎頭罐

西晉（公元265～316年）

高17.4、口徑11.7、底徑10.2厘米

平口，短直頸，溜肩，鼓腹，下腹斜收，平底。肩部飾有三圈陰綫刻紋，中間夾一圈編織紋，並飾對稱的橋形繫和虎頭以及虎尾。虎頭刻畫生動，毛髮、鬍鬚用陽綫表示，豎耳，怒目圓睜，呲牙唎齒。器身施青釉，有流釉現象。

一六三　越窰青瓷虎子

西晉（公元265～316年）

高21.3、口徑6.6、長25.3厘米

口略敞，直頸，器身呈啞鈴狀，腹下有踞臥狀四足。器身背部飾一虎形提梁。虎昂首，嘴微張，圓目外突，兩耳直豎，四肢緊抓背部，下顎鬍鬚呈芭蕉葉狀貼飾於器上，尾部呈棍棒狀貼於後部，虎背脊骨突兀，用短綫刻畫斑紋。虎的整體造型呈蓄勢待發狀，刻畫極爲生動。施青釉，微呈淡黃，釉層飽滿，釉色富有光澤，局部釉面有細小開片。值得一提的是，直接用虎身做提梁的虎子比較少見。

一六四　越窰青瓷虎子

西晉（公元265～316年）

高16.7、口徑6.7、長25.7厘米

口略敞，短頸，器身呈啞鈴狀。背部爲橋形提梁，其上飾斜方格紋。提梁一側爲虎頭，虎目圓睜，豎耳，毛髮用斜綫刻畫，另一側爲捲曲虎尾。腹下置四獸足。施青釉，釉色富有光澤，釉面有細小開片。

一六五　越窰青瓷盤口壺

西晉（公元265～316年）

高21.1、口徑13.3、底徑11厘米

蕭山城南聯華村出土

盤口，直頸，溜肩，鼓腹，下腹弧收，外底略向內弧凹。兩側貼對稱橋形繫，繫上飾有葉脈紋，前後貼飾鋪首，以弦紋夾飾寬帶狀斜方格紋。施青釉。

一六六　越窰青瓷雙繫罐

西晉（公元265～316年）

高20.7、口徑16.3、底徑10.7厘米

口略敞，圓唇，短縮頸，廣溜肩，鼓腹，下腹速收，平底。肩部兩側飾對稱半環形繫，前後貼飾唧環鋪首，並飾以弦紋夾斜方格紋。施淡黃色青釉。

一六七　越窰青瓷盆

西晉（公元265～316年）

高10.8、口徑25.9、底徑12.7厘米

平唇，略折沿，深弧腹，外底呈扁圓餅狀。口沿下飾一圈寬帶狀斜方格紋。器型規整，胎呈青灰色，外底部有支燒痕。通體施青釉，胎釉結合緊密，釉色圓潤而富有光澤。

一六八　越窰青瓷四繫罐

西晉（公元265～316年）

高14.4、口徑10.4、底徑11厘米

盤口，圓唇，短直頸，溜肩，鼓腹，下腹弧收，平底。肩部飾四個對稱橋形繫，以帶狀連珠紋夾弦紋，兩組弦紋中間再飾以斜方格紋。施青釉，釉色青中閃綠，光亮如漆，釉面布滿細小冰裂紋。

一六九　越窯青瓷貝紋四繫罐

西晉（公元265～316年）

高15.8、口徑11.7、底徑9厘米

直口，短頸，溜肩，鼓腹，下腹斜收，平底。肩上飾三圈弦紋，置四個對稱的橋形繫。繫與繫之間有貝殼形貼飾較為少見。施青釉，釉色光滑圓潤。

一七〇　越窯青瓷四繫罐

西晉（公元265～316年）

高21.2、口徑16.1、底徑12.2厘米

盤口，圓唇，縮頸，溜肩，鼓腹，下腹弧收，外底略內凹。四個橋形繫和四個鋪首貼飾分佈於肩部。口沿下有折稜紋，肩部還飾有連珠紋和夾弦紋，兩組弦紋中間再飾斜方格紋。施青釉。

一七一　越窯青瓷四繫罐

西晉（公元265～316年）

高9.8、口徑2.6、底徑7厘米

口微斂，圓唇，廣圓肩，鼓腹，下腹弧收，外底略內凹。四橋形繫分隔肩部的蓆紋，蓆紋上下各有一組弦紋。施青釉，不及底。

一七二　越窯青瓷盤口壺

西晉（公元265～316年）

高27.6、口徑15.2、底徑13.4厘米

盤口，直頸，廣圓肩，腹斜收，平底。肩部置雙複繫，前後有龍紋貼飾，繫與貼飾之間用斜方格紋填充。施青釉。

一七三　越窯青瓷盤口壺

西晉（公元265～316年）

高19.1、口徑9.2、底徑8.2厘米

盤口，束頸，鼓腹，底略內凹。肩置箭羽紋和雙繫，前後貼飾模印鋪首啣環，飾連珠紋夾斜方格紋。施青釉，有流釉現象。

一七四　越窯青瓷雙繫扁壺

西晉（公元265～316年）

高21.5、口徑9、底徑11.4厘米

圓直口，器身呈橢圓形，底平，圈足外撇。肩部飾一對狗面貼飾和一對獸頭繫，形象生動。器上部用連珠紋夾菱形紋為主，每個菱形紋內又有許多小凹點組成。施青釉。

一七五　越窯青瓷熏爐

西晉（公元265～316年）

高6.9、口徑9.3、底徑8.8厘米

直口，溜肩，扁鼓腹，下腹急收至底，平底，底足外撇。口上捏塑兩個對稱豎耳，肩、腹部各有一週圓形鏤孔。施青釉。

一七六　越窯青瓷手爐

西晉（公元265～316年）

高8.7、口徑7.8、底徑10.6厘米

斂口，口上貼塑"T"形鋬手，斜肩，圓深腹，平底。肩、腹部飾弦紋數道。施青黃釉。

一七七　越窯青瓷硯

西晉（公元265～316年）

通高8.1、口徑9、蓋徑11厘米

圓形，直口，淺折腹，平底，三獸足。硯面露灰褐色胎，有多處支燒痕。底飾弦紋數道，足似跪熊。施青黃釉。

一七八　越窯青瓷三足硯

西晉（公元 265～316 年）

高 4.3、口徑 23.4、底徑 23.2 厘米

圓形，直口，淺折腹，平底，三獸足。硯面露灰褐色胎，有支燒痕九處。底部邊緣飾兩道弦紋，置熊形足。施青釉。

一七九　越窯青瓷三足硯

西晉（公元 265～316 年）

高 3.3、口徑 11.5、底徑 11.3 厘米

圓形，直口，淺折腹，平底，三獸足。硯面露灰褐色胎，有支燒痕九處。底部邊緣飾兩道弦紋，置熊形足。施青釉。

一八〇　越窯青瓷盤

西晉（公元 265～316 年）

高 5.1、口徑 17.6、底徑 16.2 厘米

平口，直腹，平底，三獸足。獸足渾厚圓潤，穩重大方。盤腹刻弦紋。內底中央刻三週凹弦紋，內壁近底處兩條凸弦紋間有十三個扇形格，格間以凸稜相隔，每格上方與凹弦紋之間的位置都刻有數條弧綫。外底飾弦紋。施青釉，泛黃。

一八一　越窯青瓷竈

西晉（公元 265～316 年）

高 14、長 28 厘米

船形。臺面前後設大小兩口鍋臺和一個圓形出煙孔。鍋砌入鍋臺，與鍋臺渾然一體。臺面後部起翹。火膛口為長方形，火膛中空，膛口對應的臺面上豎有封火墙狀矮擋墻。施青釉。

一八二　越窯青瓷竈

西晉（公元 265～316 年）

高 11.6、長 24.8 厘米

形如尖頭靴。臺面前後設大小兩口鍋臺和一個三角狀出煙孔，後部翹起。鍋臺內各置一鍋，兩鍋被三條橫向菱形紋帶分隔。火膛口近圓形，火膛中空，無底。器身施青黃釉。

一八三　越窯青瓷豬圈

西晉（公元 265～316 年）

高 9、口徑 13.8 厘米

蕭山城南聯華村出土

圓筒形。前部開一方形口，右側上端有一長方形清掃缺口。圈外口沿飾有一道弦紋，一週豎條紋表示柵欄。圈內站有一豬，面對送食窗，豎耳，睜目，神形畢肖。通體施青釉。

一八四　越窯青瓷豬圈

西晉（公元 265～316 年）

高 5.1、口徑 13.5、底徑 11 厘米

圓形，柵欄式。圈口為直口圓唇，口部缺口處為投食口。投食口下圈內置一有把豬槽。其對面臥一豬，作正欲起立狀。豬鼻子、眼睛和耳朵用綫條勾勒，生動逼真，豬蹄、尾巴與肚臍也都表現得恰到好處。投食口處刻幾道凹綫。施青黃釉。

一八五　越窯青瓷豬圈與茅廁

西晉（公元 265～316 年）

高 9.3、口徑 15.4、底徑 13.6 厘米

豬圈為圓形圍墻，圍墻中間有一週圓形鏤孔，圈內一豬立於豬槽旁，欲吃食。茅廁一側搭建於圍墻之上，另一側以干闌式支柱支撐，墻為圓形，缺口處為出入口，置四角攢尖頂。屋頂的屋脊用凸稜表現，瓦壟刻出細綫，四角起翹，寫實感極強。施青黃釉。

一八六　越窯青瓷狗圈

西晉（公元 265～316 年）

高 3.6、口徑 11.6、底徑 8.5 厘米

狗圈爲碗形，口微斂，圓唇，淺腹稍鼓，平底。圈中央有一狗，四條腿蜷縮在一起，尾巴捲起於後腿，擡頭，兩眼圓睜，兩耳豎起。用細刻綫和戳點表現毛髮等細部特徵。通體施青黃釉。

一八七　越窰青瓷羊

西晉（公元 265～316 年）

高 7.2、長 8 厘米

山羊昂首站立，兩目圓睜，嘴巴微閉，角和耳朵向後豎起，鬍子掛於脖頸，尾巴翹起，四足蹬地。整體上圓潤美觀。施青釉，肚皮和四足露胎。

一八八　越窰青瓷鵝（兩件）

西晉（公元 265～316 年）

高 6.2、長 8.5 厘米

一鵝豎直頸脖，一鵝引頸向前。身體肥碩，用簡練的綫條刻出翅膀和尾翼，並鏤刻出眼睛、鼻孔，造型憨態可掬，極富藝術感。通體施青黃釉。

一八九　越窰青瓷竹筒形雞籠

西晉（公元 265～316 年）

高 10.2、長 13 厘米

整體爲橫置圓柱體，平底。正面左右各開一扇門和兩扇窗，正中鏤出四個倒三角孔。屋頂有屋簷，下置臺階。籠頂臥一隻雞，昂首翹尾。另有一隻雞從門口探出頭來。施青釉，底及兩側均露胎。

一九〇　越窰青瓷井

西晉（公元 265～316 年）

高 12.8、口徑 8.4、底徑 11.7 厘米

斂口，低領，折肩，筒腹，平底。肩部通施菱形紋，內壁有製坯時留下的旋痕。施青黃釉。內壁及底均露胎，外底留

有一圈支燒痕。

一九一　越窰青瓷穿帶扁壺

西晉（公元 265～316 年）

高 14.4、口徑 4、底徑 10 厘米

直口，溜肩，扁腹，六繫，橢圓圈足外撇。腹部兩側各有三繫，對稱爲上腹一繫、下腹並排雙繫，繫孔可上下穿帶。肩部自上而下飾菱形紋和一週聯珠紋，扁腹兩面均飾有大渦紋和聯珠紋，上腹部中央塑一啣環龍首，好似一龍在翻江倒海。施青黃釉。

一九二　越窰青瓷槅

西晉（公元 265～316 年）

高 5、長 17.2～12、底 19.1～13.4 厘米

方唇，淺直腹，平底，鋸齒形方圈足。底分九格，兩側大小差不多，中間方格特大。施青釉。

一九三　越窰青瓷酒具

晉（公元 265～420 年）

盤高 8.5、口徑 33.2、底徑 29 厘米

蕭山城廂鎮北幹山採集

一洗兩耳杯一勺同時出土。盤爲捲唇、淺腹、平底，器型規整而寬大，通體施青釉，釉層均勻，外底亦施釉，僅露內外兩圈支燒痕。耳杯有兩個，放於盤中正好，造型、大小相仿，口沿兩端凸起、中間稍凹，深腹，平底，雙扁耳貼於杯身中段上方，細長而向外凸出，施青釉，底部無釉。勺爲敞口，尖底，彎把，施青釉，尖底處露胎。

一九四　越窰青瓷洗

晉（公元 265～420 年）

高 6.8、口徑 18.7、底徑 9.1 厘米

斂口，寬折沿，鼓腹，平底內凹。口沿飾一週水波紋，腹部在兩條凹弦紋之間

飾一週斜方格紋帶。內底中央塑一蛙,向外紋飾依次有凹弦紋和兩週水波紋。內外施青釉,釉層不勻,有流釉現象,外底露胎。

一九五　越窯青瓷榼

東晉咸和八年(公元 333 年)

高 3.4、口徑 22、底徑 22.9 厘米

圓形,直口,平肩,平底。內外兩口之間被均分爲六個扇形格,內圈被"T"形凸稜分成三格。外底有銘文兩列,左書"咸和八年大歲癸巳九月謝夫人"、右書"虞氏榼"。施青釉,釉層較厚,施釉不均勻。

一九六　越窯青瓷洗

東晉咸和八年(公元 333 年)

高 9.6、口徑 34、底徑 19 厘米

斂口,折沿,弧腹,平底矮圈足。口沿上飾一週水波紋,內底飾有弦紋、火焰紋和水波紋。外底有銘文,左爲"虞氏",中間應爲"咸和八年大歲癸巳謝夫人"。施青釉,釉流及底,底部露青灰胎。

一九七　越窯青瓷榼

東晉(公元 317~420 年)

高 4.9、口徑 22、底徑 23.9 厘米

圓形,直口,平肩,平底,圈足。內外兩口之間被均分爲八個扇形格,內口被"T"形凸稜分成三格。施青釉,有多處土銹,底露胎。

一九八　越窯青瓷蛙形尊

東晉(公元 317~420 年)

高 13.1、口徑 12.9、底徑 10.1 厘米

敞口,高直頸,鼓腹,外底內凹。口沿有七點醬褐釉彩斑,頸部飾弦紋,安兩個對稱的橋形繫。腹部一側貼飾蛙的頭部和兩前肢,另一側爲蛙的尾巴和兩後肢。

整體施青釉,釉質圓潤透亮,有細小開片。

一九九　越窯青瓷雞首壺

東晉(317~420 年)

高 21、口徑 10、底徑 10.7 厘米

盤口,束頸,溜肩,鼓腹,平底。肩部兩側捏塑兩個環形繫。肩前置一雞頭,矮冠,珠目,尖喙,張嘴。肩後設彎棒狀把與壺口相連。施青釉。

二〇〇　越窯青瓷雞首壺

東晉(公元 317~420 年)

高 21.6、口徑 8.5、底徑 14.3 厘米

蕭山衙前鎮山南村出土

盤口,束頸,溜肩,鼓腹,平底內凹。肩部兩側安兩個對稱橋形繫。肩前置一雞頭,昂首,長頸,豎冠,珠目,圓喙中空通腹。後部壺柄高出盤口,並與壺口相連。施青釉,泛黃。底部無釉,有八處支燒痕。

二〇一　甌窯青瓷雞首壺

東晉(公元 317~420 年)

高 18.7、口徑 8.7、底徑 11 厘米

盤口,束頸,溜肩,鼓腹,平底。肩部兩側置兩個對稱橋形繫。肩前塑一雞頭,直頸,豎冠,珠目,尖喙。後部壺柄高出盤口,並與壺口相接。口、柄、繫等多處有褐色點彩。施青黃釉。

二〇二　青瓷龍柄雞首壺

東晉(公元 317~420 年)

高 23.8、口徑 9.8、底徑 12.6 厘米

盤口,束頸,溜肩,鼓腹,平底。肩部兩側飾兩個橋形繫。肩前置一雞頭,矮冠,長目,管狀喙較短且中空,並與腹相通。肩後有一龍形柄,龍頭高出盤口,龍嘴啣住壺口。施青黃釉,不及底,有開片。

二〇三　德清窯黑釉雞首壺

東晉（公元317～420年）

高14.4、口徑6.8、底徑9.5厘米

盤口，束頸，溜肩，雙繫，鼓腹，平底。肩部前置一雞首，豎冠，長目，圓喙較短。肩部後有柄高於盤口，並與壺口相接。施黑褐釉。

二〇四　越窯青瓷雞首壺

東晉（公元317～420年）

高20.2、口徑6.6、底徑10厘米

盤口，束頸，溜肩，雙橋形繫，鼓腹，平底。肩部前貼塑一雞首，鋸齒形高冠，珠目，尖喙，長頸，兩撇鬍鬚向外。肩部後有粗柄高於盤口，並與壺口相接。施青釉。

二〇五　越窯青瓷八繫盤口壺

東晉（公元317～420年）

高18.8、口徑11、底徑9.2厘米

盤口，束頸，溜肩，四複繫，鼓腹，平底。八片覆蓮花瓣自肩垂至腹部，花瓣以綫條勾勒。每隔一個花瓣置一橋形複繫。施青釉，不及底，釉色光亮。

二〇六　越窯青瓷雙繫筒形罐

東晉（公元317～420年）

高14.7、口徑11、底徑11厘米

斂口，圓唇，折肩，筒狀深腹，平底。上腹貼飾雙橋形繫。施釉不均匀，色青黃，內壁和底部露胎。

二〇七　越窯青瓷虎子

東晉（公元317～420年）

高17.9、口徑7、底徑12.1厘米

敞口，短頸，球腹，平底。短頸上方塑一虎頭，球腹上方捏飾一半環狀提梁。腹部兩側用簡單綫條和戳點刻出虎身。施青釉。

二〇八　越窯青瓷虎子

東晉（公元317～420年）

高17.2、口徑5.4、底徑11.5厘米

敞口，粗短頸，球腹，平底。環狀提梁橫跨於頸部和腹部上方。腹部刻畫簡單弧綫。施青釉。

二〇九　越窯青瓷唾壺

東晉（公元317～420年）

高16.1、口徑12、底徑13.1厘米

蕭山北幹山出土

盤口，束頸，溜肩，垂腹，平底。底爲餅狀，有支燒痕。通體施青黃釉。

二一〇　越窯青瓷點彩唾壺

東晉（公元317～420年）

高9.7、口徑8.2、底徑8.8厘米

盤口，束頸，溜肩，垂腹，餅狀底。口沿、頸部和腹部均有黑褐色點彩。底露胎，有支燒痕。施青釉。

二一一　越窯青瓷褐彩六繫盤口壺

東晉（公元317～420年）

高24.8、口徑13.2、底徑9.7厘米

盤口，束頸，溜肩，鼓腹，平底內凹。口沿、肩部和腹部均有多處褐色點彩。肩部飾六個橋形繫，前後各一，左右各一複繫。施青釉，不及底，底足露胎。

二一二　越窯褐斑點彩罐

東晉（公元317～420年）

口徑9、高8、底徑7.9厘米

直口，短頸，廣圓肩，鼓腹，下腹弧收，餅狀底。口沿上飾有一圈較繁密的褐色小斑點，肩部也有稍大的褐色斑點。肩部飾有弦紋和水波紋，腹部也飾有一組弦紋。施青釉，略顯黃色。

二一三　越窯青瓷簋

東晉（公元 317～420 年）

口徑 18.5、高 10.8、底徑 13 厘米

斂口，深弧腹，高圈足外撇。口沿下有一圈斷斷續續的連珠紋，再飾以不連貫的細麻布紋。圈足沿上有稜紋。通體施青釉，釉色圓潤有光澤，釉面有細小開片。支燒點在圈足沿上。底有銘文。

二一四　青瓷虎子

南朝（公元 420～589 年）

高 19.1、口徑 7、長 27.5 厘米

整體造型呈臥虎俯身仰首狀。圓形大直口，開口斜向上，粗直頸較短。口沿下刻朝天鼻、珠狀目和渦形耳，頸部刻條紋表示鬃毛，虎身中後略收，前腹肥壯，身上捏飾半圓形繩狀提梁，底置四臥足。施青釉，色偏黃，有開片。

二一五　青瓷虎子

南朝（公元 420～589 年）

高 24.7、口徑 6.5、長 24.2 厘米

整體造型爲臥虎俯身仰首狀。圓形直口，開口斜上，粗長頸，口沿下刻出虎頭、仰天鼻、珠狀目、渦形耳和大口，頸部刻條紋以示鬃毛，身長，中後略收，前胸肥碩，身上捏飾環狀提梁，底置四臥足。施青黃釉，有細小開片。底足無釉。

二一六　青瓷二俑竈

南朝（公元 420～589 年）

高 8.3、長 15.3 厘米

平底，長方形，上塑竈臺及二俑。竈臺分火膛和竈臺兩部分。方形膛口，膛中空，口內置柴火三根。旁邊塑一跪坐童子，高冠束角，呈填柴燒火狀。竈臺上口對應處塑山花式擋火墻，後置大小兩口鍋和小圓形出煙孔，後端翹起，小鍋內置一斷柄

勺。竈臺旁立一女俑，頭髮挽起於兩側，雙手持棒狀物搗於一盆，似在攪拌食物。通體施青黃釉。

二一七　青瓷二俑竈

南朝（公元 420～589 年）

高 8.8、長 12.3 厘米

火膛口爲拱門式，膛上封火墻式擋墻與竈臺分隔，膛內中空，口置兩根柴火。一側置一敞口鼓腹高瓶，另一側貼墻塑一俑，作添柴狀。竈臺上前後置兩口鍋和一個出煙孔，後端呈鳥尾狀翹起。後鍋內置一勺，前鍋上又放一蒸籠，上有尖頂鍋蓋。旁邊貼塑一立俑，雙手扶案。通體施青黃釉。

二一八　青瓷蓮紋盤

南朝（公元 420～589 年）

高 3.9、口徑 22.2 厘米

口略敞，圓唇，淺弧腹，平底。盤內刻出八蓮瓣，並有複瓣，中間刻出蓮蓬，內有蓮子五顆。蓮瓣上五凸點似水滴，形象生動。施青釉，有剝釉。

二一九　越窯青瓷盤龍罌

唐（公元 618～907 年）

高 45.1、口徑 22.1、底徑 13.5 厘米

盤口，縮頸，溜肩，略鼓腹，下腹弧收，平底。頸肩部置弧形四繫。一龍盤繞於繫與頸肩部，昂首平視，龍爪曲張，鱗飾呈圓珠狀。施青黃色釉，釉不及底。

二二〇　越窯青瓷盤龍罌

唐（公元 618～907 年）

高 41.2、口徑 20.2、底徑 11.2 厘米

盤口，長頸，溜肩，鼓腹，平底，假矮圈足。肩頸處捏飾四繫。頸部飾盤龍，龍爪著肩，龍身繞頸，張牙舞爪。施青黃釉，色偏紅。

二二一　越窯青瓷錢氏墓地界碑
唐貞元十八年（公元 802 年）

長 43.4、寬 27.7、厚 3.8 厘米

界碑頭部呈齒形，下部爲長方形，碑身厚重。碑文有七列，共計百餘字，介紹了錢氏的祖籍、祖輩和墓地的範圍等。施青釉，釉色圓潤光潔，釉層起泡。

二二二　越窯青瓷墓誌銘
唐大和六年（公元 832 年）

長 29.3、寬 24、厚 2.2 厘米

長方形，形體厚重。墓誌自右至左竪刻十二列，共計百餘字，介紹墓主人生平、子女及墓地範圍等。通體施青釉。

二二三　越窯青瓷缽
唐（公元 618～907 年）

高 10.7、口徑 21.2、底徑 9.1 厘米

斂口，捲沿，鼓腹，急收至底，小平底。內底、外底均有墊燒痕跡。通體施青黃釉。

二二四　越窯青瓷帶流罐
唐（公元 618～907 年）

高 5.6、口徑 11.5、底徑 5.7 厘米

斂口，捲沿，鼓腹，平底。管形流，口略高於罐口。通體施青黃釉。

二二五　越窯青瓷墓誌罐
唐（公元 618～907 年）

高 25.9、口徑 11.1、底徑 8.5 厘米

由蓋、身兩部分組成。蓋爲覆蓮狀、蓮瓣口，鈕爲寶珠狀，鈕下爲蓮葉。器身較長，圓角方口，方筒腹，平底。器身四面均刻有字，爲墓誌內容，叙述了余氏的生平和一些家事。通體施青黃釉。

二二六　越窯青瓷雙耳罐
唐（公元 618～907 年）

高 14.5、口徑 12.3、底徑 7.3 厘米

敞口，溜肩，弧腹，平底。肩部貼飾雙耳。內外施青黃色釉，釉層均勻光亮。

二二七　越窯青瓷注子
唐（公元 618～907 年）

高 9.8、口徑 4.6、底徑 3.7 厘米

喇叭口，束頸，溜肩，深腹稍鼓，矮圈足。肩部飾一瓜稜形短流，另一側置扁條形把。施青釉，釉色光亮異常。整體造型清瘦挺拔，極具美感。

二二八　越窯青瓷注子
唐（公元 618～907 年）

高 8.6、口徑 1.1、底徑 3.6 厘米

蕭山北幹山出土

小斂口，葫蘆形腹，上小下大，管狀彎流自下腹向上斜起，扁條形把，平底。施青釉。

二二九　青瓷圈足硯
唐（公元 618～907 年）

高 4.4、口徑 16.6、底徑 20 厘米

圓形，餅形硯面凸出，高圈足外撇，圈足上鏤有如意雲紋。施青釉。

二三〇　越窯青瓷雙繫罍
唐（公元 618～907 年）

高 32.8、口徑 13.9、底徑 9.5 厘米

盤口，束頸，溜肩，鼓腹，平底。口部飾有弦紋，起折稜，肩頸結合處置對稱半環狀雙繫。施青釉，不及底。

二三一　青瓷粉盒
唐（公元 618～907 年）

高 7、口徑 11.5、蓋徑 12.8 厘米

拱形蓋，子母口，直腹，近底處急收，平底。滿施青釉，均勻柔和。

二三二　青瓷碗

唐（公元618～907年）

高5.1、口徑15、底徑6.6厘米

敞口，深弧腹，玉璧底。素面無紋。通體施青黃釉，釉層潔淨光亮。

二三三　越窰青瓷盤龍罌

唐天祐三年(公元906年)

口徑13.9、高28.9、底徑8.3厘米

盤口，弧縮頸，溜肩，鼓腹，下腹斜收，平底，圓矮假圈足。頸肩部有四繫，盤龍貼塑於繫與頸肩部。龍首平視，咧嘴，尖齒外露，彎角上蹺，卵形珠目外突，形象生動。背脊扁平直豎，圓珠狀鱗，以斜方塊形表現健碩肢幹，龍爪三前一後，塑於器物上。通體飾青釉。腹部一側有銘文“天祐三年七月八”。

二三四　越窰青瓷粉盒

五代（公元907～960年）

高2.7、口徑8.4、蓋徑9.6、底徑5.2厘米

拱形蓋，子母口，淺腹，平底。通體施青釉，釉層均勻。

二三五　越窰青瓷粉盒

北宋（公元960～1127年）

高6.2、口徑12、蓋徑13.3、底徑9.6厘米

蕭山城南東蜀山出土

拱形蓋，子母口，弧腹，圈足外撇。蓋上刻有花草紋、弦紋等。通體施青釉，光亮明淨。

二三六　越窰青瓷罐

北宋（公元960～1127年）

高9.1、口徑6.1、蓋徑5.6、底徑7.7厘米

笠式蓋，置小紐，斂口，球腹，圈足外撇。蓋及腹部均刻有花草紋。通體施釉，色青灰。

二三七　越窰青瓷鳥形哨

北宋（公元960～1127年）

高4.3、長5.5厘米

整體造型爲抽象、簡化的鳥。鳥首刻出眼睛，尖嘴等。身爲球腹、小平底，腹部一側斜向上伸出尾部。三個圓形口於腹部成三角形分佈。器身有多組細綫刻紋。通體施青黃釉。

後　記

　　蕭山古陶瓷可以追溯至距今八千年的跨湖橋文化遺址出土的陶器。蕭山有明確考古學證據的古代製陶業上迄春秋，下止南朝，有著一千三百多年的歷史，是蕭山積累最厚的歷史文化財富。作爲中國瓷器的發源地之一，展示蕭山這張具有特殊意義的歷史文化名片，是我們文博工作者多年來的心願。蕭山博物館在籌建之初，就將古陶瓷列爲博物館的主題內容，並計劃陳列商周時期以來的印紋硬陶、原始瓷器和東漢至隋唐時期的越窰青瓷三大類型，以此來揭示蕭山在中國瓷器出現、發展與成熟過程中所具有的特殊地位。《蕭山古陶瓷》一書就是在這樣的背景下開始編寫的。

　　本書在編寫過程中，得到了中國古陶瓷研究會副會長、國家文物鑒定委員會委員、南京博物院研究員張浦生先生的大力指導。他多次親臨蕭山，無償爲博物館鑒定古陶瓷藏品，還爲此書擔任顧問並作序。浙江省博物館副館長李剛先生、浙江省文物考古研究所副所長陳元甫先生和沈岳明先生以及復旦大學文博系教授朱順龍先生等也多次來館幫助與指導，在此深表謝意！

编　者

2006 年 10 月

赵心波

儿科临床经验选编

现代著名老中医名著重刊丛书

中国中医研究院西苑医院儿科 整理

第一辑

人民卫生出版社
People's Medical Publishing House

内容提要

全国著名老中医赵心波先生有五十多年的临床医疗经验，尤其擅长治疗儿科疾病。在临床证上，他既注意辨证与辨病相结合，又注重摸索疾病的治疗规律，善于以温病学理论指导治疗小儿传染病与发热性疾病，在治疗神经系统疾病及调治小儿脾胃疾患等方面，多有独到之处。

全书分两部分。前一部分为儿科常见疾病证治，介绍了赵先生对34种儿科常见病的辨证论治、处方用药经验，每病均以病因病机、辨证分型、常用方药、治疗思路儿方面进行论述；后一部分为医案，载述赵先生经治病案90余则，分别按病况、立法、方药、治疗过程、按语予以记录。书中还收录了赵先生生常用的13首中成药验方。本书内容精练实用，方法简明有效，是一本不可多得的中医儿科名医经验集。

责任编辑／王立子
封面设计／李暌
版式设计／何美玲
责任校对／吴小翠

赵心波 儿科临床经验选编